Blood
Wedding

Blood Wedding

Federico García Lorca
Translated by David Johnston

Hodder & Stoughton

A MEMBER OF THE HODDER HEADLINE GROUP

Performance Rights

Order queries: please contact Bookpoint Ltd, 39 Milton Park, Abingdon, Oxon
OX14 4TD. Telephone: (44) 01235 400414, Fax: (44) 1235 400454.
Lines are open from 9.00-6.00, Monday to Saturday, with a 24 hour message answering
service. Email address: orders@bookpoint.co.uk

British Library Cataloguing in Publication Data
A catalogue record for this title is available from The British Library

ISBN 0340 51269 5

First published 1989
Impression number   18 17 16 15 14 13 12 11
Year   2001 2000 1999

Typeset by Keyset Composition, Colchester, Essex.
Printed in Great Britain for Hodder & Stoughton Educational,
a division of Hodder Headline Plc, 338 Euston Road, London NW1 3BH
by Athenæum Press Ltd, Gateshead, Tyne & Wear.

Acknowledgments

I should like to express my gratitude to the Carnegie Trust for the Universities of Scotland for the generous financial support which enabled me to undertake a visit to Madrid and Granada during the preparation of this book. I also welcome this opportunity to record publicly my thanks to the following people: Gerry Mulgrew (and through him the actors who took part in Communicado's production of *Blood Wedding*) for his marvellous sense of *duende*, Karen Wimhurst for the hauntingly beautiful music which she composed for the songs of the play, Heather Baird and Maggie MacKay (also of Communicado) for their constant help with reviews, photographs, etc.; John London for his helpful suggestions when the manuscript was still in its infancy; and, especially, Marisé for communicating to me in the most direct way possible the whole sense of what Lorca is all about.

Introduction

Lorca and Andalusia

On 22 July 1928, in the dusty heat of the Andalusian province of Almería, a young bride abandoned her husband-to-be on the very morning of their wedding day to elope with her childhood sweetheart. In this society, where the obsession with reputation and honour has been sharpened by prolonged contact with successive waves of Islam and inquisitorial Catholicism, retribution was both swift and violent. An ambush was laid, the lover was shot dead and the wayward bride strangled and left for dead by her own sister, outraged at the public disgrace brought upon the family name. The people of the village of Níjar, where the events had taken place, closed ranks and drew a heavy veil of silence over the whole affair, a silence which has remained unbroken until of late.[1] The incident did stir some passing interest in both the local and national press but, like nearly all news items of a similarly sensational nature, just as quickly slipped from public memory. It seemed that the 'crime of Níjar', as it had been rapidly dubbed, would be forgotten by all but those who had actually experienced the tragic events at first hand. It was at this point, however, that the creative imagination of Federico García Lorca intervened, re-interpreting the whole incident in line with the most

---

[1] It was not until 15 October 1985, when Spain's national newspaper *El País* carried an account of a travelling theatre company's performance of *Blood Wedding* in Níjar, that Casimiro Pérez Morales (the 'Bridegroom' of the incident) broke a silence which had lasted nearly sixty years. Both Casimiro and Francisca Cañada Morales (the 'Bride'), perhaps understandably, refused to attend the performance. Although living in the same village, they have had no contact with each other since 1928.

fundamental preoccupations of his own work and producing, as he did so, a play which ranks as an acknowledged classic of world theatre.

Quite clearly, Lorca's initial interest in the 'crime of Níjar' was fired by the sheer drama of the events themselves, by what he would have considered the intensely Andalusian feel of a story of overflowing passions and revenge. It is precisely this feeling for the Andalusian, that special sense of place inspired by a tradition that is markedly different from that of the rest of Spain, which gives Lorca's work its own very distinctive voice. In an interview published in 1934, just a year after the hugely successful Madrid première of *Blood Wedding*, Lorca described the pull of the land in his work:

> I love the land . . . All my emotions are closely tied to it. My most distant childhood memories all have a taste of earth. The earth, land, have had an enormous influence on my life. Insects, animals, the ordinary people of the land, all have a richness which is perceived by only a few. But I remain open to it with the same intensity as when I was a child. Otherwise, I could never have written *Blood Wedding*.

The land of Andalusia is always present in the work of Lorca. It provides the physical setting for whole books of poems, like *Gypsy Ballads*, as well as for the trilogy of rural tragedies, of which *Blood Wedding* was the first, and it is transformed into a deeply felt absence in the wasteland of urban life, as Lorca perceived it in his *Poet in New York*. The elements of the land, as he observed and experienced them on an everyday basis in and around his birthplace of Fuentevaqueros, in the province of Granada, become the dominant symbols of his work, and the Andalusian landscape itself is poetically transformed into a vast theatre in which the forces of life and death are in constant confrontation.

So land and the sense of the land give Lorca's work both its central arena of action and its obsessive themes. By talking with those who worked in the fields or by just simply observing, the young Federico was irresistibly drawn into the continual struggle to produce life in the midst of arid desolation, towards the intense joy inspired by any oasis of fertility in that part of Spain where greenery no sooner bursts into life than it is consumed under the burning sun. It is not hard to see from this why green becomes the primary colour in the palette of a writer whose extraordinary sensitivity to colour and strongly visual imagination were born in the heightened perceptions of the play of light on land. Nor is it difficult to understand why green for Lorca signals both life's intensity and its fragility, that all too fleeting moment of blossom before the inevitability of rapid decay. It may indeed be that the vaguely tragic sense that Lorca describes in his poems as having beset him since childhood has its origins in the young boy's most direct experience of the land. And in the lecture which he wrote to accompany public readings of his *Gypsy Ballads* he describes what he believes is a childhood memory (although he does admit the possibility that it was a purely imagined encounter) which was crucial for his subsequent development, both as an artist and as a man:

> I was eight years old and playing at home in Fuentevaqueros when another boy suddenly looked in through the window. He seemed a giant, and he glared at me with a scorn and hatred that I shall never forget. Just as he moved to go, he spat at me, and I heard a distant voice calling: 'Amargo, come on! Come on, Amargo!'
>
> After that, this Amargo grew inside me until at last I understood why he had looked at me like that – an angel of death and of the despair that guards the doors of Andalusia. The figure has become an obsession in my poetic work.

The name 'Amargo' means 'bitter one', and Lorca was later to write three poems in which he presents the 'Amargo' as one of the key figures of his whole work. In these poems the figure is characterised by both his swaggering embrace of life and an unswerving instinct for death, so that he comes to stand in Lorca's mind for the complex of emotions inspired by the contemplation of life's fragility. One of these poems, 'Song of Amargo's Mother', was later to be partially transformed into the words spoken by the Mother in the final scene of *Blood Wedding*. Moreover, the fact that Amargo is stabbed to death in one of these poems is immediately reminiscent of the knife with which the play opens and ends, the dominant symbol which presides over the whole action so that even the malignant moon–character is presented as a 'knife hanging in the air'. If the knife is Lorca's own version of the Damoclean sword hanging over all of humanity, then the 'Amargo' is the embodiment of his awareness that death is most violent when life is at its most intense. The whole of Lorca's work becomes in equal parts a celebration of life, especially of passionate life, as D. H. Lawrence would have understood it, and a keen lament at the brutal inevitability of death.

The awareness of death which suffuses Lorca's work can be clearly felt to have its initial origins in the everyday experience of life on the land. Here death is simply a familiar part of life, and we can perhaps understand the appearance of the 'Amargo' to the young Federico as the sudden burgeoning of this 'peasant' reality in the boy's hitherto cosseted bourgeois existence.[2] The images of death, and especially of violent death, which recur constantly in Lorca's work, therefore, are rarely gratuitous and are always felt to be part of the process of life itself. There may well be some sense of that 'black and baleful Spanish obsession with death' in Lorca, as the

---

[2] Paul Binding, *Lorca: The Gay Imagination* (London: GMP, 1985, especially pages 31–32). This is one of the most interesting books to have been published on Lorca in English in recent years. Deservedly, it has just been translated into Spanish.

[3] Hamish Henderson, 'Lorca and *Cante Jondo*', *Cencrastus* (Summer 1987, pages 6–10). This piece is particularly interesting in its attempt to describe some sort of cultural and linguistic equivalent in English for Lorca's *duende*.

Scottish writer Hamish Henderson has suggested.[3] But it is a vision of darkness which does not negate life, but rather highlights it, always being geared towards the intensity of experience that springs from the awareness that our days are numbered. It is precisely this dangerous but exhilarating challenge to a death foretold which is ritualised in the bullfight. And that is why, just a few months before he was to meet his own violent end, Lorca was to declare that the bullfight 'is the most cultured festival in the world today . . . the source of our greatest poetry and vitality', although he himself was by no means a seasoned *aficionado*.

The *duende*

In one of his most revealing and suggestive lectures, 'Theory and play of the *duende*', first delivered in Buenos Aires in 1933, Lorca attempted to define this dark presence in his art in terms of the *duende*. Meaning literally 'lord of the house', the *duende* has passed into Spanish folklore as a puckish figure capable of intervening, for better and for worse, in the lives of ordinary mortals. Lorca, however, uses the word in a much more strictly Andalusian sense, one which is more intrinsically linked to the tradition of flamenco music than anything else. Here it refers to that mysterious, perhaps indefinable power in a singer or dancer which transforms great technical prowess into great art. We might perhaps understand this in terms of the dionysian lifeblood which can transfigure both the singer and the song, but in any event Lorca certainly saw the *duende* as the shiver of response produced in the listener or spectator by the projection of emotional intensity against the constant awareness of death's inevitability. For Lorca the *duende*, this 'mysterious power that everyone feels but which no philosopher can explain', comes from the power to peel back layers of restraint so that the quick of our emotional being is laid bare. The *duende* re-orientates the listener or spectator towards the deepest root of his or her being:

> So the *duende* is a power and not an action, a struggle and not a thought. I have heard an old guitar maestro say that the *duende* is not in the throat, but that it surges up inside you right from the soles of the feet.

This renewed suggestion that it is our physical contact with the earth – in the sense of our ability to respond naturally and fully to sensual experience – which unleashes the disturbing force of the *duende* within us finds a vital echo in *Blood Wedding*. Towards the end of the play, as Leonardo tries to come to terms with the forces which have caused him to rebel against everything he has been brought up to hold sacred, he simply says that 'It's not me who's to blame, it's the earth itself'. This really states the crux of Lorca's sense of life. The passionate and sensuous responses of Lorca's characters spring from the deepest parts of their being, from their condition as creatures of the land, but they are responses which draw upon themselves the full hostility of a society which has organised itself so as to minimise the full force of individuality. When he read of the 'crime of Níjar', therefore, Lorca would have immediately seen in the incident a potent image of the conflict between the non-codified responses of the individual, where the *duende* is to be found, and the strictures of a rigidly codified society. The fact that the urgent bid for freedom of the unfortunate bride and lover should have ended in violent death would have further heightened Lorca's painful sensitivity to the short-lived moment of human fulfilment.

Lorca always insisted that the culture of Spain in general, and that of Andalusia in particular, was especially receptive to this tragic sense of life:

> Throughout the ages Spain has been moved by the *duende*, for it is a land of ancient music and dance where the *duende* squeezes the lemons of dawn – a land of death.

> A land open to death . . . Everywhere else death is an end.
> Death comes, and the curtains are drawn. But not in
> Spain. In Spain they are opened. Many Spaniards live
> indoors until the day they die, and only then are they
> taken out into the sun. A dead man in Spain is more alive
> than anywhere else in the world. His profile wounds like
> the edge of a barber's razor . . . Throughout the country,
> everything finds its final, metallic value in death.

The 'land of ancient music and dance' is really a specific
reference to the Andalusian tradition rather than to the
majority Spanish culture – or cultures, given the
enormous historical diversity of the various peoples who
co-exist, at times uneasily, in the Spanish State. In
particular, it refers to what the non-initiated would
consider to be the flamenco tradition, the musical form
through which Andalusian identity finds its most
forceful cultural expression. Lorca, however, makes a
vital distinction between flamenco and *cante jondo*, or
deep song. In very broad terms, flamenco is an
eighteenth-century consequence of *cante jondo*, which is
one of the very first manifestations of song, its origins
lying in the primitive musical systems of India. In Lorca's
own words, while flamenco is relatively modern, deep
song 'is imbued with the mysterious colour of primeval
ages'.

With the encouragement of the great composer
Manuel de Falla, Lorca had devoted himself both to
collecting the traditional songs of Andalusia and to
reworking and re-creating them in his own artistic image,
frequently incorporating some of the most lyrical imagery
bodily into his own work. The way in which Lorca
transposes the heavily imagistic language of Andalusia
and of Andalusian song into his plays, in particular *Blood
Wedding* and *Yerma*, gives his work its very distinctive
voice. Lorca takes the speech of his community,
especially in its manifestations in the popular culture of
songs, ballads and sayings, and distils it to an essence of
imagery and metaphor, creating a dramatic language

which is simultaneously poetic and familiar. Perhaps no one Andalusian would speak with the same wealth of expression as do Lorca's characters. But a Spanish audience would immediately recognise and respond to the powerful sense of a community voice that the playwright has vested into each and every one of those characters.[4]

But the tradition of deep song was more than a popular source which lends colour to Lorca's dramatic language. Lorca's meeting with Falla, when the future dramatist was still a young student, was to have profound repercussions for his artistic development and cultural awareness. Falla's best-known compositions, such as 'Nights in the Gardens of Spain' and 'Love Bewitched', are highly dramatic pieces in which the techniques and styles of the modern tradition of Ravel and Stravinsky are combined with popular, indeed ancient, elements inherited from the Andalusian tradition. In a broad sense, this is exactly what Lorca does in his work and it explains why such a theatrically innovative play as *Blood Wedding* is also full of the echoes of a timeless folk culture. Falla quickly recognised Lorca's genius, both as a potential musician and as a poet capable of revitalising Andalusian popular culture, and in guiding his pupil towards the musical roots of that culture he gave him his first and most abiding insight into the Andalusian heart of darkness which the figure of the 'Amargo' clearly represents.

Lorca very quickly produced a book of poetry – *Poem of Deep Song* – whose central purpose was to give open

---

[4] The writer that Lorca has most frequently been compared to in this respect is J. M. Synge, and the community speech in *Blood Wedding* has been likened to the language of the Aran Islands that Synge endeavours to re-create in his *Riders to the Sea*. The dramatic language of Sean O'Casey (another, but very different, Irish playwright), which is based on the talk of Dublin tenements, would also bear close comparison to that of Lorca.

expression to this heart of darkness kept alive hitherto in popular song. The lyricism and forceful imagery which were to characterise much of Lorca's later work, and in particular the trilogy of rural dramas, are born here:

> It is both wondrous and strange how in just three or four lines the anonymous popular poet can condense the most intense emotional moments in human life. There are songs where the lyric tremor rises to a point which is inaccessible to all but a few poets:
>
>> The moon is cold
>> in its halo,
>> my love has died.

Once again, the link in Lorca's mind between emotional intensity and death is striking. We have already seen that he describes the cultural force of deep song as the *duende* squeezing 'the lemons of dawn', and here he is emphasising a form and impulse which are simultaneously creative and destructive. Living is squeezed to the maximum, but the bitter cup remains to be drunk. In *Poem of Deep Song* he dedicates a single poem to the singer Juan Breva, whose voice he describes in similar terms as possessing the quality 'of a sunless sea and an orange squeezed dry'. This is the essence of the deep song tradition from which Lorca clearly saw his own work and preoccupations as deriving, and to which he longed to make a meaningful and lasting contribution. Our point of access into this imagery is perhaps through the emotional resonance (what Lorca called the 'lyrical tremor') of the words. Both art and life – in the sense of Bergson's *élan vital* or urgent, passionate life – spring from the compressing of experience, from savouring the sensuous intensity which, for Lorca, was the essential dimension of human living. But this sweetness is thrown into sharp perspective by the foreboding presence of death, a 'sunless sea' which contains within itself its own beginnings and ends.

The dark struggle

Through deep song, therefore, Lorca found a wider cultural mirror for his own artistic and existential preoccupations. In the poem already mentioned Lorca talks about Juan Breva as 'sorrow itself singing behind a smile', and there can be little doubt that this is how, in point of fact, he actually saw himself. Everyone who came into contact with Lorca, at any stage of his life, was always greatly struck by the vivacity of his personality, by his playful nature and apparently inexhaustible *joie de vivre*. However, Vicente Aleixandre, the poet who won the Nobel Prize in 1977 and one of Lorca's closest friends, has this to say on the subject:

> His heart was certainly not a happy one. He was capable of all the happiness under the sun; but in his deepest being, perhaps like any great poet, he knew no happiness. Those who watched him fly through life like a brightly coloured bird simply did not know him. His heart was capable of a passion that few could equal, a capacity for love and for suffering that ennobled his already noble being.

A factor which clearly would have contributed to Lorca's unhappiness, at least as a young man, was the fact of being homosexual in a distinctly male-dominated society – it is no accident that we still use the Spanish word for 'maleness' (machismo) to refer to this particular ethos. More than anything else, as his first poems, which are his most personal and confessional pieces, movingly reveal, this accounts for his sense of feeling himself to be outside the flow of life itself. Both society and nature seemed to have rejected him, and his own deepest-rooted feelings and desires only served to confirm in his own mind what he considered to be the grotesqueness of his condition. Small wonder then that sexuality and death should remain so closely wreathed in Lorca's consciousness.

However, he quickly kicked over the traces of this imposed attitude – although it is known that he always bitterly regretted his inability to talk openly with his sternly conventional mother about his sexuality. He came to terms with the feelings at work within him, learning to accept them as no less a force of nature than the animals on the land or the fertility of the fields. And so, rejected by social convention, he in turn began to reject those same conventions. Society in Lorca's mind becomes identified, in a very Freudian way, as an oppressive mechanism which locks away, indeed threatens, the primal responses of human beings, and which does them untold psychological damage. Nowhere is this sense of repression voiced more powerfully than in *Yerma*, in which the protagonist laments how her desires and her frustrations are forcibly contained within the immediate four walls of her home, the only legitimate arena of social action for women in the rural Spain of Lorca's time:

> Some things never change. There are things locked away behind these walls which won't change because nobody knows they're here . . . But if they all suddenly broke out and screamed, then they would fill the whole wide world with their shrieks.

It requires little imagination, in the light of this, to understand why Lorca should have sympathised to the extent that he did with the gypsies of Andalusia, both as a marginalised group and as a community opposed, virtually by definition, to the stifling conventions of his own bourgeois world. Moreover, the gypsies were not simply another persecuted group – although persecution certainly was, and to some extent continues to be, a basic reality of their everyday experience of life. When Lorca explained that he had chosen the gypsies as the vitalistic protagonists of his *Gypsy Ballads* because 'the gypsy is the . . . very keeper of the glowing embers, of the blood and alphabet of Andalusian and universal truth', he was thinking of the gypsies as the people who, towards the end of the first millennium, had brought deep song into Spain from India via North Africa and who still preserved its forms in their greatest purity. And if deep song was for Lorca the ancient expression of the primitive consciousness hemmed in by a growing sense of limitations, of the life urge dashed against the blank wall of impossibility, then the gypsies became the modern inheritors of that consciousness, honest and urgent in their living, but perhaps inevitably doomed.

In this sense, Lorca saw his task as essentially one of redefining what is meant by civilisation, and, in particular, of identifying that area which civilisation concedes to the primal impulses, of which the erotic is both the most representative and the one which best lends itself to a fully dramatic treatment. Lorca saw clearly how the dead hand of socialisation – meaning the trained and inculcated responses which make us apparently fit members of society – sits heavily upon the passionate self – that is, the dark part of the human animal that most intimately identifies us as elements of the natural world. And, once again, he found that this sense, which he evolved through his own hard personal experience, was also a living issue of Andalusian history. For several hundred years, until well into the fifteenth century, the Arab province of al-Andalus had been undoubtedly one of the most genuinely civilised parts of Europe. The so-called liberation of Granada by Ferdinand and Isabella, the Catholic Kings, in 1492, marked the final re-unification of Spain and the culminaton of the fervent sense of mission which had galvanised the various Christian kingdoms in Spain up until then. It is a date sacred to Spanish traditionalists – in fact the rhetoric of the Catholic Kings five centuries later was ably enlisted to the cause of Francoism – a date which, for Lorca, sounded the death knell of an admirable and unique civilisation.

However, the continued cultural presence of deep

song, which he fought desperately to maintain, convinced Lorca that the sensuous delicacy and emotional intensity of a long-disappeared civilisation had not in fact been totally lost. Instead, it had been sublimated deep within the Andalusian consciousness, just as the marvellous mosque in Córdoba had been overlaid by a Gothic fortress cathedral or Charles V's imperial quarters had intruded into the sensual splendour of the Alhambra, the palace built by the Moors in Granada. All of Lorca's work centres relentlessly, perhaps obsessively, upon what he called the 'dark struggle' between this sublimated consciousness and the socialised self, a struggle which is perhaps best understood in terms of the continual duel between the luxuriant art of the Moors and the austere architecture of the new Catholic Spain. In his early poetry up until and including *Gypsy Ballads*, published in 1928, this 'dark struggle' is projected into the cultural categories of the ancient music of a timeless Andalusia lurking just under the surface of the present moment, in the same way perhaps that the eternal gypsy in us lies just beneath the social self. The approach is broadly synchronic, and we can sense that in the creation of a poetry that is both situated in a broad conflict of cultures rather than a particular moment of history and expressed through the motifs and myths of an ancient culture, Lorca is both distancing himself from his own immediate pain and seeking consolation for it. Andalusia becomes the timeless arena in which the universal battle is fought. Perhaps the struggle is waged with more intensity here than in other parts, but its reference is to all times and all places. But Lorca was soon to be forced to sharpen the focus of the struggle.

The nightmare of New York

Towards the end of 1928 various pressures of a personal nature, including the burden of his own fame, made Lorca decide to undertake a period of residence outside Spain. In 1929 he set off to spend nine months in the United States, largely in New York, stopping briefly in England on the way. It was his experience in 'the geometry and anguish' of a New York just about to undergo the financial trauma and human nightmare of the Wall Street Crash which, in the broadest of senses, shocked him into a more specific engagement with the immediate historical moment. The timeless Andalusian landscape, echoing with the stylised flamenco cry, was far away, and although several of the poems that Lorca wrote in New York derive from his love of myth, especially perhaps that of innocence found and lost, the young Spanish writer was suddenly immersed in a world whose potent blend of unfamiliarity and immediacy produced the strongest of reactions in him. The result was *Poet in New York*, a powerful, at times surrealistic, indictment of the urban nightmare and spiritual desolation of New York, a bleak diagnosis of the illnesses of the Western world that has been frequently likened to Eliot's *Wasteland*.

On one level, the crisis that Lorca underwent in New York was an aesthetic one. The very traditional forms, which had previously provided Lorca with a vehicle for distancing his own private obsessions and concerns, now seemed inadequate for expressing his growing concern with the particularly modern problem of what he saw as 'the painful slavery of man together with machine'. Moreover, both his immediate identification with the life of the land and the sense of cultural integration, which were formative elements in his earlier work and which made the use of popular forms possible, were absent in his experience of life in the New World. Lacking what we might call the objective correlative, or distancing element, of the Andalusian tradition, Lorca was increasingly subjectivised by life in New York.[5] The result is a verse form which is difficult precisely because the central springboard of experience is not New York itself, but the nightmare of New York, that is, Lorca's highly personal and subjective account of his vision of a city 'imperfect in its despair'.

This crisis of form clearly goes hand in hand with a sharpening of Lorca's awareness of the social implications of the central theme of his work. In New York he had glimpsed, he felt, the future awaiting the whole Western world, and his conscience as a poet and as a human being would not allow him to create a literature which did not stir to anger. In one of the key poems of the collection, 'New York. Office and condemnation', the poet signals a new commitment to protest:

> What should I do then? Impose form on a country view?
> Impose form on loves that will later be photographs,
> and then pieces of wood, then mouthfuls of blood?
> No, no; I condemn.
> I condemn the conspiracy
> of these deserted offices
> marooned so far from pain,
> offices which sweep the jungle from us,
> and I offer myself up to be devoured
> by bruised and battered cattle
> when their cries fill the valley
> where the Hudson flows, drunk on oil.

Lorca has not changed his view of life, nor his belief that the most precious fulfilment of human nature lies in the honest recognition of one's innermost impulses (hence the condemnation of a mechanistic system and materialistic ethos 'which sweep the jungle from us'). But, under the pressure of immediate circumstances, lament has become attack.

---

[5] See Binding (op. cit.), especially pages 77–78.

Another factor which underlies this development was the rise of European fascism. In a curious way, Lorca's alienation in the United States sensitised him to the implications of what was taking place in Europe, granting him a perspective which otherwise might only have come with the force of much later events. The Concordat, signed in 1929 between Mussolini and Pope Pius IX, in the name of the Italian Catholic Church, convinced Lorca that rigid traditionalism, with the dogma-sanctioned violence that it breeds, was much more than the dark side of the perennial problem of the individual's existence in any given social framework. It was an urgent issue which called for an immediate response. In this case his response was channelled most completely into 'Cry to Rome (From the Chrysler Building)'. Here his fear that 'nothing remains but a million smiths/forging chains for the children still to be born' heralds the commitment to what he was later to call his 'theatre of social action', the theatre that he was to set about creating upon his return to Spain. But it also betrays what is perhaps his ultimate pessimism, his final fear that there is no longer anything that can be done and that the human cry for freedom can only degenerate into a lingering scream of impotence and frustration (both meanings are implicit in the original Spanish *grito*). It is this movement from the cry to the scream, from the break for freedom to final defeat, which encases the whole action of *Blood Wedding*, the first major play which Lorca was to undertake upon his return to Spain.[6]

---

[6] In this respect, see Eric Bentley, *Life of the Drama* (London: Methuen, 1965, especially pages 278–279).

Back to earth

In the last five years of his life, between 1931 and 1936, Lorca devoted increasing time and energy to the theatre. During that time he still managed to write some very fine poetry, including the beautiful sequence published under the title of *The Divan of Tamarit*, but theatre began to dominate his life. It is certainly true to say that his theatrical activity prior to his stay in New York gave little indication of this latter development. Lorca's plays written before *Blood Wedding*, with the notable (but not entirely successful) exception of *Mariana Pineda*, were largely short pieces whose immediate inspiration lay in Andalusian puppet theatre and, more indirectly, in the tradition of *commedia dell'arte*. Several of these early pieces had received a mixed press, to say the least, but upon his return from New York Lorca dedicated himself to theatre with a commitment and an energy which suggested that he had indeed been born to the stage.

In 1931 Lorca accepted an appointment from the Republican Government. His brief was, no more, no less, that of bringing the acknowledged classics of Spanish theatre, and especially the masterpieces of the great trilogy of dramatists of the Golden Age – Lope de Vega, Calderón and Tirso de Molina – to the remote villages of the country. The company that Lorca formed to carry out this commission, La Barraca (meaning 'the stall' or 'the hut'), was immensely successful and formed a clear turning-point, at least for a time, in popular acceptance of the nation's classical theatre. The motif of the company was a circle divided into a double-sided face, simultaneously smiling and weeping in the time-honoured style. But when Lorca defined theatre as 'a school for laughter and tears' he was doing much more than paying homage to its Janus-like gaze towards comedy and tragedy alike. He was stressing that through theatre people could once again experience those emotions which everyday living dulled and destroyed or which society encouraged them to repress. In a similar manner, he devised his own plays – in particular, the rural tragedies – as a point of access for his audience so that they could feel and respond to the burning frustration of pent-up emotion and the cathartic freedom of release.

There is no doubt that it is the emotional force of Lorca's writing which constitutes the great strength of his theatre. His characters are driven wholly by their passions, both positive and negative, rarely, if ever, stopping to analyse their responses so that they seem to be transformed into forces of nature struggling with imposed sterility rather than individual human beings in debate with their circumstances. These are people who speak from the centre of their being, from that point where the unstoppable drive of passion and the immovable force of tight-lipped convention co-exist in explosive tension. The build-up of imagery in these plays, and most clearly in *Blood Wedding* and *Yerma*, is geared towards communicating to the audience, in the most direct way possible, the relentless force of the emotional drives which Lorca saw as governing human life. To understand how this works, especially if our experience of the play is to be limited to the printed page, it is perhaps useful to develop the inspired reference that Stephen Spender makes to Lorca's 'grammar of images'.[7]

By this the English poet means that Lorca's dramatic language possesses a notable coherence of symbolism and imagery. It is a coherence maintained by the fact that the individual elements which are woven into the images, symbols and metaphors which form the rich linguistic fabric of his plays are drawn in large part from the observation of daily life on the land of Andalusia – horses, walls, knives, water, blood, trees, etc. Moreover,

---

[7] See Binding (op. cit.), especially page 51.

these are easily identified with elemental and natural forces – the horse, for example, can be readily associated with male power and therefore, by analogy, with male sexuality – so that they touch deep within the spectators' consciousness, pushing them towards a reaction which is wholly emotional rather than reflective. In this respect, we would perhaps be hard pushed to think of another major playwright of our century whose theatre is more diametrically opposed to Brechtian theory. Be that as it may, all of these elements become long-term emblems in the play, recurring constantly and obsessively, so that the audience is increasingly struck by the sense of elemental forces running through the play, pushing and pulling the lives of the characters. These long-term emblems could well be likened to the syntax of Lorca's grammar. In *Blood Wedding* the two most notable emblems are 'blood' and 'knife' (with its variants of dagger, wedding pins, sharp glass, etc.), and these two recurrent motifs intertwine to evoke in the most powerful way Lorca's abiding sense that the intensity of life (the pulsing of the blood) is constantly menaced by, indeed co-exists with, inhumanity and death (knife, the flowing of blood).

This sense of two elemental and mutually antagonistic forces implicit in the emblem of blood is central to the whole meaning of *Blood Wedding*, creating an unresolvable tension in virtually every image and every metaphor so that each manages to speak simultaneously of both life's glory and its end. It is this tension which Lorca believed would summon up the *duende* of the play, a tension which vibrates in the work from the first moment. Indeed, it is already suggested by the title. The wedding of blood suggests the passionate union of two lovers (the relationships between the Bride and Bridegroom, and Leonardo and the Wife, which are more socially acceptable but also much less dynamic, are, therefore, frequently presented through the emblem of water). But the reference to blood is also a dark intimation of the blood that will inevitably be spilt. This duality is echoed, in particular, by the imagery of the songs, so that these serve to heighten the tension of this confrontation between elemental forces. In this way the songs are perfectly integrated into both the structure and the meaning of the play, and their dominant images are wholly linked to the structures of long-term emblems in which the play's action is encased. So that while it is quite plausible to sing a cradlesong about a horse reticent to drink, even about a horse with a dagger in its eye (violent images of this nature are curiously present in the lullabies of many cultures – we only have to think about the choppers which threaten to come along to chop off babies' heads in English songs), the audience cannot fail to respond to the sense of foreboding implicit in the song. When it is resumed after the angry departure of Leonardo, the parallel is clear. Leonardo is the horse who cannot drink at the water of marriage, and the dagger in his eye is both an image of self-mutilation, his attempt to kill an illicit but genuine love, and a further intimation of his violent death.

The fact that Leonardo feels constrained to repress this passion (later on in the play he talks in similar terms of throwing sand into his eyes) is important. There is a widely held misconception that Lorca's characters are wholly passionate beings, children of a wild universe who rebel as a matter of course against the social order. Nothing could be further from the truth. Lorca's protagonists are not revolutionaries. They are all socially responsible people who, at least initially, accept the social status quo. This permits the dramatist to locate the 'dark struggle' within the character, rather than solely pitting the character against society. When society finally turns its full fury on to the figure who has broken away, as it also did in Níjar in 1928, it is only after the force of the character's welling passions has submerged his or her strength of will. In a sense, through all of his major characters – Leonardo and the Bride in *Blood Wedding*, Yerma, and Adela in *The House of Bernarda Alba* – Lorca reworks and broadens the implications of his own early struggle as a homosexual, torn between the responses inculcated in him by convention and his desire to give full rein to his own nature. It is perhaps relatively easy to see from this why Lorca should have felt himself increasingly drawn to dramatising the specific problems faced by women in society. The conceptual framework of his work remains the same as before, but now Lorca's heightened awareness of social crisis, which was the main element in the artistic baggage he brought back from New York, leads him to consider the specific problems faced by concrete people in identifiable circumstances. Lorca turned to the position of women in a male-dominated society, in part because he saw it as a terrible injustice in its own right, in part because the tragedy of women forced to conform to standards of behaviour actively hostile to their real needs is a version of the great human tragedy of love locked away behind the wall of public façade.

This explains why *The House of Bernarda Alba*, the all-female play which marks the culmination of this, is described by its author as a 'drama of women in the villages of Spain'. *Blood Wedding* does portray the terrible solitude of women in this society with genuine power and compassion, in its final scene especially. But this, the first play of the trilogy, is more fundamentally concerned with depicting the tragedy of love baulked by both materialism and the fervent acceptance of society's most relentlessly violent responses (embodied by the Father and the Mother respectively). In this world, marriage is simply a social contract, a ritual which celebrates community life over individual freedom, material gain over human fulfilment. But beyond this network of destructive social circumstances, the switch in dramatic key at the start of Act 3 brings into play the tragic sense at the heart of Lorca's vision of life, namely that the whole impulse of the universe is hostile to human fulfilment. The scene in which the bloodlust of the Moon allies with the perverse sensuality of Death, presented in folk terms as a Beggarwoman, to conspire jointly against the fleeing lovers is one of the most powerful moments in Spanish theatre. To see it on stage is to experience, intimately and deeply, the shivering passion of Lorca's *duende*.

Yerma followed *Blood Wedding* in 1934. In this 'tragic poem' Lorca shows how a natural impulse – in this case, the maternal instinct – sours into obsession and finally flares into violence when it is frustrated. Denied a child by her materialistic husband, Yerma feels that he has flaunted the unspoken contract which governs marriage in this traditional society. In the terms in which she has been brought up, she is a good, submissive and caring wife. And in return, as she has been led to believe, she will be elevated to the status of motherhood. When Yerma kills her husband at the end of the play, therefore, she is avenging what is essentially his refusal to stick to his side of the bargain. In her perception, by breaking the rules, he has betrayed her as grievously as would an unfaithful wife her husband. But in a society accustomed to Calderonian responses on the part of men, anxious to restore face, Yerma's killing of her husband was considered actively subversive. For it was not simply inspired by madness, but was rather the action of a woman who had fully accepted the social and sexual status quo and who had applied the ultimate sanction of that status quo – the killing of the unfaithful woman – against her own husband. Spanish traditionalists were never to forgive Lorca.

The House of Bernarda Alba was finished on 19 June 1936. Less than one month later the Civil War began to flare throughout Spain as General Franco undertook his 'crusade' to rid Spain of the plague of liberalism. And less than one month after that, under the direct orders of the Nationalist Military Governor of Seville, General Queipo de Llano, Lorca was executed just outside Granada by a paramilitary firing squad and laid to rest in an unmarked grave. He was killed because, above all else, he had been a champion of freedom, a defender of the underdog. He had once written that 'being born in Granada has enabled me to understand and feel for all those who suffer persecution – the Gypsy, the Black, the Jew and the Moor which all Granadans carry inside them'. Statements like this and the evidence of plays like *Blood Wedding* and *Yerma* (*The House of Bernarda Alba* was not to receive its first performance until 1945, in Buenos Aires) were enough to convince the authorities that the poet Lorca was politically dangerous. Ian Gibson, his biographer, who has also written the most accurate account of Lorca's last days, concludes simply that, in the final analysis, Lorca was assassinated 'by an attitude of mind'.[8] It was that same attitude of mind, that rigidly codified response to the world, which Lorca had poured into the character of Bernarda Alba, the mother who imposes the sterility of prolonged mourning on her daughters just as, perhaps, his own mother's attitudes had imposed a form of metaphorical mourning on him. The last word that she speaks in the play, and one of the last words that Lorca was to write for the theatre, was the prophetic 'Silence!'. For nearly forty years all the rest was, indeed, silence.

David Johnston
Glasgow, June 1989

---

[8] Ian Gibson, *The Death of Lorca* (St Albans: Paladin, 1974, page 142).

Note to this translation

This translation began to take shape in Madrid during the months of April and May 1988. It was always conceived of as a script for performance rather than solely a text to be read, although this should not be understood as a green light for 'translator's licence'. Rather it means that the translator must ensure, above all other things, that the final product works as a play on stage and not solely on the page. No play is easy to translate in this way. But perhaps Lorca presents particular difficulties.

The main problem in both translating and presenting Lorca derives from the same area which is also his greatest strength as a dramatist, that is, from the fact that his characters speak from the very centre of their being, and that his is in essence a theatre of poetry and emotion. The rich imagery and beautifully interwoven strands of symbolism which form the linguistic fabric of Lorca's plays, the highly charged *Blood Wedding* foremost among them, are all geared towards the communication of a restless passion which an English-speaking spectator may simply dismiss as excessive. Lorca's Spanish is a powerful vehicle for emotional tension and striving passion, straying uncaringly into the realm of melodrama just as consciousness frequently wanders into fantasy and dream. The English language, while perhaps not quite wholly unable to express sheer emotion on stage, certainly does tend more to resort to the sort of finely graded nuances of meaning which hint at shades of feeling. This is a difference which is both linguistic and cultural, and accordingly the translator must make certain degrees of linguistic and cultural concession. In this sense, translating Lorca's *Blood Wedding* involves treading a delicate path between respect for a play which is perfectly balanced in the original, and the awareness that the reactions of an English-speaking audience are most certainly not those of a Spanish one.

Lorca's plays, especially the three rural tragedies, are constructed on the basis of what we might call long-term and short-term imagery. As noted in the introduction, the long-term imagery provides the syntax of what can be usefully seen as Lorca's 'grammar of images'. In the case, for example, of the description of the tongue 'run through and through with sharpest glass', glass clearly represents the invasion of the inhuman, the mutilation caused to the self by the cold process of socialisation. The idea of it piercing the tongue is an explicit echo of the action of the knife, the most forceful long-term image in the play. This is the type of understanding upon which these concerted image structures must be translated. In other words, they must be both translated and, where necessary, partially explained in a way which is in keeping with the other emblems within the image structure. The short-term imagery of the plays really equates to the telling, suddenly vivid image in normal discourse. The basic effect of this type of image is to suggest a quick swell of emotion within the speaker, the source of which he or she is very often only remotely aware, or which the speaker seeks to repress, so that the image works on virtually a subliminal level.

To cope with this the translator must create his or her own grammar of images to correspond to that of Lorca, clarifying or adding in the interests of clear cultural transposition, but always within the framework of that grammar. This occurs most frequently in the case of *Blood Wedding* when the translator is faced with song or poetry. Literal translation here, especially when one is working with a composer, is impossible. And yet, by working within this grammar, it is possible to be totally faithful to the original in terms of its dramatic impact, which is what the art of drama translation is really all about. It is this imagistic vein of expression which invests the plays with their characteristic force – a power of expression which, allied to Lorca's characteristically tragic sense of life, creates a fierce energy which is the driving force of Lorca's plays, the *duende* of the work. The translator must avoid the twin dangers of ascent into the rarefied heights of a consciously poetic diction – the danger for those who misunderstand that Lorca's dramatic genius resides in his ability to create that dimension of poetry which is theatre's alone – or descent to the kind of picturesque sensationalism that an English-speaking audience might very well expect from a Spanish play. Lorca's *duende* lives very much in the real world. His language is intensely poetic, but poetic almost in an everyday way. His images and figures of speech are drawn from a heightened vein of everyday language and have to receive the same treatment in English, otherwise the impact is lost.

The upshot of all of this is that while this translation cannot claim to be wholly faithful to every last letter of the original Spanish (although, in every case where it can be, it is), it does strive to re-create as far as possible the *force* of Lorca's dramatic world. In the event, the translation was first performed by Communicado Theatre Company, under the direction of Gerard Mulgrew, in the Lyceum Studio at the 1988 Edinburgh Festival, where the production won the prestigious Edinburgh Festival *Scotsman Award*. Both Gerard Mulgrew, who is one of the most stimulating and innovative directors at work in British theatre today, and his talented cast convinced this translator at least that it is possible to capture and re-create the intensity of Lorca's language, and communicate what his work is really about without leaving an English-speaking audience with the comfortable and very mistaken impression that Lorca's plays are simply picturesque windows into a culture whose essential problems are a world away from their own.

David Johnston
Glasgow, June 1989

Blood Wedding

A Tragedy
in Three Acts
and Seven Scenes

Cast List
(in order of appearance)

Bridegroom
Mother (of the Bridegroom)
Neighbour
Mother-in-law (of Leonardo)
Wife (of Leonardo)
Leonardo
Young Girl
Maid (to the Bride)
Father (of the Bride)
Bride
Wedding Guests
Woodcutters
Moon
Death (as a Beggarwoman)
Girls from the village
Women in mourning

ACT 1 ◆ *SCENE 1*

A room painted yellow.

BRIDEGROOM *entering* Mother.

MOTHER Yes?

BRIDEGROOM I'm going now.

MOTHER Where?

BRIDEGROOM The vineyard. *He makes to leave.*

MOTHER No. Wait.

BRIDEGROOM What?

MOTHER Son, take some food with you . . .

BRIDEGROOM Don't worry. I'll eat grapes . . . get me
the knife.

MOTHER What for?

BRIDEGROOM *laughing* To cut them.

MOTHER *muttering as she looks for it* Damn the knife,
damn them all and the devil who brought them into
the world . . .

BRIDEGROOM Just forget it.

MOTHER Knives . . . guns . . . pistols, even the sickle
and the scythe . . .[1]

BRIDEGROOM All right . . .

MOTHER Anything that can slice through a man's
body. An angel of a man, in the flower of his life,
going out to the vines or the olive groves, because
they're his, his family's . . .

BRIDEGROOM *looking down* Please don't go on.

MOTHER And then he just doesn't come back. Or if he

does, it's only so that you can lay out his body, and rub it with salt so it doesn't bloat in the heat. I don't know how you can bear to carry a knife, nor why I even have one in the house at all, like a snake in my kitchen.

BRIDEGROOM   You've said enough.

MOTHER   If I were to live another hundred years I couldn't say enough. First, your father, who filled me with the scent of carnations . . . for three short years. And then, your brother . . . How can something so small, a gun, a knife, bring down a bull of a man? And you say I've said enough? The months trail past, and the pain still stings my eyes and pulls at my hair . . .[2]

BRIDEGROOM   *emphatically*   That's enough!

MOTHER   No, no, it can never be enough . . . Can anything ever bring back your father? Or your brother? And people talk about prison. What is prison? They still eat there, they smoke there . . . they even have music there. And my two dead boys lie silent, slowly filling with grass, turning to dust; two men who were like two flowers . . . and their killers, cool and fresh in prison, gazing at the mountains . . .

BRIDEGROOM   What do you expect me to do? Kill them?

MOTHER   No . . . It's just . . . every time I have to watch you go through that door, carrying a knife, how can I not say something? I wish you didn't have to go out to the fields.

BRIDEGROOM   Oh, come on . . .

MOTHER   I wish you were a woman. So you wouldn't have to go off to the river now, and we could settle down here to talk and sew . . .

BRIDEGROOM   *taking his* MOTHER's *arm, and*

laughing   Mother . . . what if I took you down with me to the vineyard?

MOTHER   And what would you do with an old woman like me in the vineyard? Just lay me down under the vines?

BRIDEGROOM   *lifting her up in his arms*   What an old, old moan you are![3]

MOTHER   Your father really did use to take me, you know . . . He was so strong . . . good blood. Your grandfather only had to look at a woman and she would fall pregnant. That's the way it should be. Men . . . life . . .[4]

BRIDEGROOM   And my life, Mother?

MOTHER   Your life?

BRIDEGROOM   Do I need to tell you again?

MOTHER   *serious*   Ah!

BRIDEGROOM   But, are you against it?

MOTHER   No.

BRIDEGROOM   Well then?

MOTHER   I just don't know . . . Whenever you spring it on me like this, it's as though I was hearing the news for the first time. I know she's a fine girl. I know she is . . ., quiet and hard-working. She bakes her father's bread and sews her own skirts, and even so, whenever I hear her name, it's like being struck by a stone.

BRIDEGROOM   But that's foolish.

MOTHER   It's not just foolish. I'll be here on my own. I've only you left and I don't want you to go.

BRIDEGROOM   But you'll come with us.

MOTHER   How can I? I won't leave your father and
         brother alone here . . . I go to see them every
         morning, and if I went away, and one of the Felix
         family died, they might put them beside them . . .
         and I'll have no murderer lying with any of mine.
         Never. Because I'd dig them up with my nails and
         teeth, and smash their bodies against the wall . . .

BRIDEGROOM   *emphatically*   Don't start again.

MOTHER   I'm sorry. *Pause.* How long have you
         known her?

BRIDEGROOM   Three years now. I've saved enough to
         buy the vineyard.

MOTHER   Three years. She had . . . there used to be
         somebody else, didn't there?

BRIDEGROOM   I don't know . . . I don't think so . . .
         anyway, girls have a right to have a good look at the
         man they're marrying . . .

MOTHER   Perhaps. But I didn't look at anyone until I
         met your father. And when the Felix murdered
         him, I looked straight ahead at the wall. One
         woman with one man, and nothing else.

BRIDEGROOM   But you've said that she's a fine girl.

MOTHER   I'm sure she is. But still, I would feel easier if
         I'd known her mother.

BRIDEGROOM   What's that got to do with anything?

MOTHER   *fixing her gaze on him*   Son . . .

BRIDEGROOM   What?

MOTHER   Nothing . . . you're right! When do you want
         me to speak to her father?[5]

BRIDEGROOM   *happily*   What about this coming
         Sunday?

MOTHER *serious* I'll take her the studded earrings, they've been in the family for generations, and you can buy her . . .

BRIDEGROOM Whatever you think best . . .

MOTHER You can buy her some embroidered silk stockings, and for yourself two new suits . . . Three . . . You're all I've got.

BRIDEGROOM I'm away now. And tomorrow I'll go and see her.

MOTHER Yes, yes . . . and remember, I expect six grandchildren, six at the very least – now that your father's gone . . .

BRIDEGROOM The first one just for you.

MOTHER Make sure that there are some girls among them, so that we can sew and embroider and be at peace.

BRIDEGROOM I'm sure you'll grow to love her.

MOTHER I'm sure I will. *She goes to kiss him and pulls back.* Away with you, you're too big for kisses now. Give them to your wife. *Pause.* When she is your wife.

BRIDEGROOM I'm going.

MOTHER Make sure you turn over the part near the mill, you've been neglecting it lately.

BRIDEGROOM Don't worry.

MOTHER And take care. *The* BRIDEGROOM *leaves. The* MOTHER *remains seated with her back to the door. A* NEIGHBOUR, *dressed in dark colours and wearing a headscarf, appears in the doorway.* Come in.

NEIGHBOUR How are you keeping these days?

MOTHER As you find me . . .

34

NEIGHBOUR   I was down at the shops, and came over to see you . . . We live so far apart.

MOTHER   It's over twenty years since I've even been to the top of the street.

NEIGHBOUR   You're just right.

MOTHER   Do you think so?

NEIGHBOUR   All sorts of things go on. Just the other day they brought home my neighbour's boy with both of his arms sliced clean off by the new harvesting machine.   *She sits down.*

MOTHER   You mean Rafael?

NEIGHBOUR   Yes, Rafael. What's he fit for now? Sometimes I think our boys are better off where they are, at rest, sleeping, rather than risking being left useless.

MOTHER   No . . . Say what you like, but there's no consolation.

NEIGHBOUR   Ay![6]

MOTHER   Ay!

Pause.

NEIGHBOUR   *sadly*   What about your son?

MOTHER   He's just gone.

NEIGHBOUR   So he managed to get the money together for the vineyard.

MOTHER   He was lucky.

NEIGHBOUR   He'll be getting married now . . .

MOTHER   *as though suddenly awakening, she moves her chair closer to that of the* NEIGHBOUR   I'd like to ask you . . .

NEIGHBOUR   *confidentially*   Go on . . .

MOTHER   Do you know my son's . . .?

NEIGHBOUR   A fine girl.

MOTHER   Yes, but . . .

NEIGHBOUR   But you couldn't say that anyone really knew her. She lives with her father, just the two of them, in the back of beyond, a good couple of hours from the nearest house. But she's a good girl. Well used to her own company.

MOTHER   What about her mother?

NEIGHBOUR   Oh, I knew her all right. Beautiful. Her face shone like a saint's, but I never did like her. She didn't love her husband.

MOTHER   *loudly*   The things people know.

NEIGHBOUR   Sorry. I meant no offence . . ., but it's true. Now, there was never any talk about whether she was a decent woman or not. Not a single word. She was so proud that . . .

MOTHER   Must you . . .?

NEIGHBOUR   Well, you asked.

MOTHER   I wish nobody knew anything about them, dead mother or living daughter, I wish they were like two thistles, untouched and forgotten, but always ready to scratch and jag if any tongue comes too close.[7]

NEIGHBOUR   Of course. You've got your son to think of.[8]

MOTHER   I know . . . That's why I'm asking. I've heard that the girl had a boyfriend . . . some time back.

NEIGHBOUR   She would have been about fifteen. He got married a couple of years ago, to a cousin of hers in fact. Everyone's forgotten the whole thing by now.

MOTHER   How is it you remember it then?

NEIGHBOUR   You did ask . . .

MOTHER   It's just like any other illness. The more you know the safer you are. Who was he?

NEIGHBOUR   Leonardo.

MOTHER   Leonardo who?

NEIGHBOUR   Leonardo Felix.[9]

MOTHER   *standing up*   Felix!

NEIGHBOUR   Woman dear, what can you possibly have against Leonardo. He'd barely turned eight at the time.

MOTHER   I know . . . But I hear the name Felix, and I feel my mouth fill with mud, Felix   *She spits.*   and I've got to spit it out, I've got to spit otherwise I'll kill every last one of them.

NEIGHBOUR   Calm down . . . This won't do any good at all.

MOTHER   No, but you understand don't you?

NEIGHBOUR   Don't stand in the way of your son's happiness. Say nothing to him. You and I are old. We must hold our peace.

MOTHER   I'll say nothing.

NEIGHBOUR   *kissing her*   Nothing at all . . .

MOTHER   *serenely*   Things . . .

NEIGHBOUR   I'm going. My men will be back from the fields soon.

MOTHER   The sun's scorching hot.

NEIGHBOUR   The lads running water to the reapers are fed up with it. I must go. God bless.

MOTHER   God bless.   *She walks towards the door stage left. Half way across she stops and slowly blesses herself.*

Curtain.

*A room painted pink, filled with gleaming copperware
and flowers. In the centre a covered table. Morning.*

LEONARDO'S MOTHER-IN-LAW *is cradling a young
child. Opposite her his* WIFE *is sewing.*

MOTHER-IN-LAW
    Hush, child, hush
    sing a song
    of the horse
    who wouldn't drink,
    of water
    that wouldn't be drunk,
    of the stream
    singing round
    little children's feet.
    Who can tell,
    my little one,
    what the water holds
    in its long tail,
    in its dark green rooms?

WIFE   *softly*
    Sleep, little flower,
    the horse just won't drink.

MOTHER-IN-LAW
    Sleep, little rose,
    the horse is weeping,
    his wounded hooves
    and poor, poor
    frozen mane,
    and in his eye
    a silver dagger shone.
    Down to the river,
    down to the stream,
    all the way down

blood flows fuller
than water.[10]

Sleep, little flower,
the horse just won't drink.

MOTHER-IN-LAW
Sleep, little rose,
the horse is weeping now.

WIFE
He lifts his head
from the water's edge
through flies and heat
with a breaking heart
to the shadow of mountains
far, far away
and so the river dies
and dries upon his throat.
Oh, the poor, poor horse
who just wouldn't drink,
in the shivering cold snow
the cold horse of dawn.[11]

MOTHER-IN-LAW
Stay, little one, stay,
pull your window to,
inside your bed of dreams
your lonely dreaming bed.

WIFE
Sleep now, sleep.

MOTHER-IN-LAW
Dream, softly dream.

WIFE
The horse lays down
his head to rest.

MOTHER-IN-LAW
> In his shining
> cot of steel.

WIFE
> On his shining
> quilt of silk.

MOTHER-IN-LAW
> Hush, child, hush.

WIFE
> Oh, the poor, poor horse
> who just wouldn't drink.

MOTHER-IN-LAW
> Stay, child, stay,
> let him run
> to the mountain side
> through valleys grey
> and mountains green
> to his young
> mare's side. [12]

WIFE *looking at the child*
> Sleep now, sleep.

MOTHER-IN-LAW
> Hush now, hush.

WIFE *very softly*
> Sleep, little flower
> the horse just won't drink.

MOTHER-IN-LAW *standing up, and very softly*
> Sleep, little rose,
> the horse is weeping now.

> *They take the child into another room. Enter*
> LEONARDO.

LEONARDO The child?

WIFE Asleep.

LEONARDO   He wasn't himself yesterday. And then he cried all night.

WIFE   *cheerfully*   He's as fresh as a rose today. What about you? Did you get the horse shod?

LEONARDO   That's just where I've come from. But it's hard to keep up with him – he's no sooner shod than he casts them off again. They must catch on the sharp stones. [13]

WIFE   Perhaps you're riding him too much.

LEONARDO   I hardly ever have him out.

WIFE   Yesterday somebody told me they'd seen you right at the far side of the flatlands.

LEONARDO   And who might that have been?

WIFE   The women picking capers. I couldn't believe it. Was it you?

LEONARDO   No. What would I be doing in that Godforsaken spot?

WIFE   That's what I thought. But the horse was wreathed in sweat.

LEONARDO   And did you see him?

WIFE   No. My mother did.

LEONARDO   Is she in with the child?

WIFE   Yes. Would you like some lemon?

LEONARDO   Make sure the water's good and cold. [14]

WIFE   If only you'd come home in time for . . .

LEONARDO   I was at the weighing station. It's a slow business.

WIFE   *preparing the drink. Tenderly*   Did you get a good price?

LEONARDO   A fair one.

WIFE   I could do with a new dress, and the baby a bonnet with some nice ribbons.

LEONARDO   I'm going in to see him.

WIFE   Try not to wake him.

MOTHER-IN-LAW   *entering*   That horse looks as if it's been ridden into the ground. It's tethered up down there, lathered in sweat and its eyes rolling in its head as if it had been to the end of the world and back. Who'd . . .

LEONARDO   *bitterly*   Me.

MOTHER-IN-LAW   Excuse me. He's yours to do what you want with.

WIFE   *timidly*   He was at the weighing station.

MOTHER-IN-LAW   He can go to the gates of hell as far as I'm concerned.   *She sits down.*

Pause.

WIFE   Is your drink cold enough?

LEONARDO   Yes.

WIFE   Have you heard my cousin's getting engaged?

LEONARDO   When?

WIFE   The two families are getting together tomorrow. She'll be married within the month. I hope they invite us to the wedding.

LEONARDO   *serious*   I'm not so sure.

MOTHER-IN-LAW   Well, I heard that his mother isn't exactly over the moon about the whole thing.

LEONARDO   I don't blame her. Your cousin needs watching.

WIFE   What have the pair of you got against her? She's never done any harm to anyone.

MOTHER-IN-LAW   Ah, but remember, Leonardo knows her well . . . at least he did.   *Pointedly.*

LEONARDO   I used to know her.   *To his wife.*   Don't start crying. Come on.   *He brusquely pulls her hands away from her face.*   Let's go and see the baby.   *They go out arm in arm.*

A YOUNG GIRL *enters, running excitedly.*

GIRL   Señora . . .[15]

MOTHER-IN-LAW   What is it?

GIRL   He's down there now, the bridegroom, down at the shops, buying the best of everything.

MOTHER-IN-LAW   On his own?

GIRL   No, with his mother. Very serious, very tall.   *Imitating her.*   Oh, the things they bought.

MOTHER-IN-LAW   There's no shortage of money there.

GIRL   Embroidered silk stockings . . . oh, they were gorgeous. The sort you can only dream about. Look: a swallow here   *indicating her ankle,*   a boat here   *indicating her calf,*   and just here . . . a rose   *indicating her thigh.*

MOTHER-IN-LAW   Child!

GIRL   Oh, a rose with its seeds and stalk. Ay! Everything pure silk.

MOTHER-IN-LAW   They're two well heeled families all right. And money breeds money . . .[16]

LEONARDO *and his* WIFE *return.*

GIRL   I came to tell you what your cousin's fiancé has been . . .

LEONARDO   What do we care?

WIFE   Leonardo, leave her be.

MOTHER-IN-LAW   There's no need to rear up at her like
      that.

GIRL   I'm sorry.   *She exits crying.*

MOTHER-IN-LAW   Why in God's name do you have to
      be so unpleasant?

LEONARDO   Did I ask for your opinion?   *He sits down.*

MOTHER-IN-LAW   Fine.

      Pause.

WIFE *to* LEONARDO   What's wrong with you? I can
      never tell what's going on inside your head.
      Please . . . please . . . it's not fair not to tell me.

LEONARDO   Leave me alone.

WIFE   No, I want you to look at me and tell me.

LEONARDO   I'm going.   *He stands up.*

WIFE   Where?

LEONARDO   *bitterly*   Why can't you just shut up?

MOTHER-IN-LAW   *forcefully, to her daughter*   Do as he
      says.   LEONARDO *leaves.*   The baby!   *She goes to
      fetch him.*[17]

      The WIFE *remains standing, as though transfixed.*

MOTHER-IN-LAW
      His wounded hooves
      and poor, poor
      frozen mane,
      and in his eye
      a silver dagger shone.
      Down to the river
      down to the stream,
      blood flows fuller
      than water.

WIFE   *turning round slowly, as though dreaming*
Sleep, little flower
for the horse
just won't drink.

MOTHER-IN-LAW
Sleep, little rose
the horse is weeping now.

WIFE
Hush, child, hush.

MOTHER-IN-LAW
Sing a song
of the horse
who wouldn't drink.

WIFE   *dramatically*
Stay, child, stay,
let him run
to the mountainside.
In the shivering cold snow
the cold horse of dawn.

MOTHER-IN-LAW   *weeping*
Sleep now, sleep.

WIFE   *weeping, slowly drawing nearer*
Dream, softly dream.

MOTHER-IN-LAW
Sleep, little flower
for the horse
just won't drink.

WIFE   *weeping, leaning on the table*
Sleep, little rose,
the horse
is weeping now.

Curtain.

ACT 1 ♦ SCENE 3

Interior of the BRIDE's *house, carved out of the rock itself.*[18] *At the back a cross of large pink flowers. Round doorways, curtained off with lace hangings tied back with pink ribbons. The walls are covered with a hard white material. Here and there are round fans, blue vases and small mirrors.*

MAID   Please come in.   *Affably full of a hypocritical humility. The* BRIDEGROOM *and his* MOTHER *come in. The* MOTHER *is wearing plain black with a lace mantilla. The* BRIDEGROOM *wears black corduroy, with a large gold chain.*   Do have a seat. They'll be with you directly.   *She goes out.*

They sit down. Motionless, like statues.

Long pause.

MOTHER   Did you bring your watch?

BRIDEGROOM   Yes.   *He takes it out and looks at it.*

MOTHER   We must be sure to get away in good time. These people live in the back of nowhere.

BRIDEGROOM   But it's good land.

MOTHER   Maybe, but too far off the beaten track. A four-hour journey, and not a single house or tree.

BRIDEGROOM   What do you expect on flatlands like these?

MOTHER   Your father would have had a tree in every corner.

BRIDEGROOM   What, without water?

MOTHER   He'd have found some somewhere. In the three years we were married he planted ten cherry trees   *recalling*   and the three walnut trees down by the mill, a whole vineyard and a Jupiter plant, the sort that gives bright crimson flowers. But it dried up. [19]

Pause.

BRIDEGROOM   *referring to the* BRIDE   She must be getting ready.

The BRIDE'S FATHER *comes in. An old man with shining white hair. He stoops slightly.* MOTHER *and* BRIDEGROOM *stand up and shake hands in silence.*

FATHER   Long on the road?

MOTHER   Four hours.   *They all sit.*

FATHER   You must have come the long way round.

MOTHER   I'm a bit long in the tooth to clamber round by the river.

BRIDEGROOM   She gets sick.

Pause.

FATHER   Good alfalfa crop this year.

BRIDEGROOM   Yes, indeed.

FATHER   When I was your age this land wouldn't even give alfalfa. We had to work it with our sweat and tears to get anything from it.

MOTHER   Now you do. But you needn't worry. I'm not here to ask you for anything.

FATHER   *smiling*   You're a wealthy woman. Vineyards are worth a fortune. Each young plant is like a piece of silver in your pocket. It's a shame that our lands, so to speak, are so far apart. I like to bring things together . . . to see them grow. There's a small plot right in the middle of my land, and all the gold in the world wouldn't persuade them to part with it . . . it breaks my heart every time I see it.

BRIDEGROOM   That's always the ways of things.

FATHER   Imagine if we could harness twenty pair of
          oxen to haul your vineyards over here, and graft
          them onto my land . . . Wouldn't it be wonderful?

MOTHER   Why?

FATHER   What's mine is hers and what's yours is his.
          That's why. To bring it all together, to grow
          together . . .

BRIDEGROOM   It would certainly mean less work.

MOTHER   When I'm gone you can sell our land and buy
          out here.

FATHER   Sell? Sell? Bah! Buy . . . buy everything you
          can get your hands on. If I had been blessed with
          sons, I would have bought everything from the
          mountains right down to the stream. It's not good
          land, but with willing arms . . . and nobody ever
          comes by here to steal your crops, so you can rest
          easy at night.

          Pause.

MOTHER   You know why I'm here?

FATHER   I do.

MOTHER   Well?

FATHER   It's fine by me. They've talked it over.

MOTHER   My son has the very best of prospects.

FATHER   My daughter is the finest of girls.

MOTHER   My son is handsome. He has never known
          any woman. As clean and pure as a sheet in the sun.

FATHER   What can I say about mine . . .? She's up at
          three, with the morning star itself, to bake bread.
          Never speaks at all, unless spoken to first; as soft
          and gentle as wool, she embroiders all sorts of . . .
          embroidery. And she can cut a rope with her
          teeth.[20]

MOTHER God bless this house.

FATHER May God bless us all.

The MAID *appears with two trays, one with glasses, the other with sweetmeats.*

MOTHER *to her son* When do you want the wedding?

BRIDEGROOM Next Thursday.

FATHER Her twenty-second birthday.

MOTHER Twenty-two! My eldest would be twenty-two if he'd lived. He'd still be alive today, warm and full of hopes, if men had never invented knives.[21]

FATHER You mustn't dwell on it.

MOTHER What else can I do?

FATHER So, next Thursday. Is that right?

BRIDEGROOM That's right.

FATHER The church is a fair distance, so we'll go with them by car. Everyone else can manage by cart or whatever else they happen to come in.

MOTHER Yes, I think that's best.

The MAID *crosses the room.*

FATHER Tell her she can come in now. *To the* MOTHER. I'm sure you'll like her.

The BRIDE *appears. Her hands are demurely folded and she stares at the floor.*

MOTHER Come to me, child. Are you happy?

BRIDE Yes, señora.

FATHER You shouldn't look so serious. After all, it's your new mother you're speaking to.

BRIDE I am happy. That's why I want to get married.

MOTHER   Of course you do.   *Taking her by the chin.*   Look at me.

FATHER   She's the living image of my wife.

MOTHER   Is she? What lovely eyes. Do you know what marriage is all about, my little one?

BRIDE   *serious*   Yes, I know.

MOTHER   It's a man and his children, and a thick stone wall to keep the rest of the world out.[22]

BRIDEGROOM   What more could you need?

MOTHER   Nothing more! You'll be so happy! Both of you.

BRIDE   I know what's expected of me.

MOTHER   We've brought you a few presents.

BRIDE   You're very kind.

FATHER   Won't you have something to eat?

MOTHER   Nothing for me.   *To the* BRIDEGROOM.   What about you?

BRIDEGROOM   Yes, I'll have one of these.   *He takes a sweet. The* BRIDE *also takes something.*

FATHER   *to the* BRIDEGROOM   A glass of wine?

MOTHER   He never touches it.

FATHER   All the better.

Pause. They are all standing.

BRIDEGROOM   *to the* BRIDE   I'll come tomorrow.

BRIDE   When?

BRIDEGROOM   At five.

BRIDE   I'll be waiting.

BRIDEGROOM   Every time I have to leave you I feel as if I've been uprooted or ripped in two, and I get this sort of lump in my throat.

BRIDE   You won't feel like that once you're my husband.

BRIDEGROOM   I know.

MOTHER   We must go. The sun won't wait.   *To the* FATHER.   Everything's agreed?

FATHER   Everything.

MOTHER   *to the* MAID   Goodbye.

MAID   God go with you.

The MOTHER *kisses the* BRIDE, *and they start to leave. Silence.*

MOTHER   *in the doorway*   Goodbye, my dear.

The BRIDE *remains silent, but acknowledges the* MOTHER *with her hand.*

FATHER   I'll see you out.

They leave.

MAID   I'm dying to see the presents.

BRIDE   *bitterly*   Leave them alone.

MAID   Oh, please, show me them.

BRIDE   I don't want to.

MAID   Even just the stockings. I've heard they're embroidered silk. Please!

BRIDE   No, I said.

MAID   For heaven's sake. Oh, all right. Anyone would think you didn't want to get married.

BRIDE   *biting her hand with rage and frustration*   Ay!

MAID   Sweetheart, what's wrong? Is her royal highness frightened that the good life is about to come to an end? Don't worry about that. There's no need. None at all. Let's have a look at what they brought you. *She snatches the box.*

BRIDE   *taking her wrists* Leave them!

MAID   You're hurting.

BRIDE   Put them down!

MAID   You've the strength of a man.

BRIDE   Haven't I always done a man's work? I wish I was one.

MAID   Why are you talking like this?

BRIDE   Forget it. We'll talk about something else.

The light is slowly fading. Long pause.

MAID   Did you hear a horse last night?

BRIDE   When?

MAID   About three o'clock, I suppose.

BRIDE   A stray runner from the herd.[23]

MAID   No, it was being ridden.

BRIDE   How do you know?

MAID   I saw the rider. He stopped right outside your window. I was shocked.

BRIDE   It must have been my . . . fiancé. He sometimes comes at that time.

MAID   It wasn't.

BRIDE   But did you actually see him?

MAID   Yes.

BRIDE   Who was it?

MAID   It was Leonardo.

BRIDE   *fiercely*   That's a lie! You're lying! He has no business to be here.

MAID   Maybe not. But he was here.

BRIDE   Shut up. Damn your tongue!

The sound of an approaching horse is heard.

MAID   *running to the window*   Quickly, look . . . Well, was it?

BRIDE   Yes! It was him.

Quick Curtain.

Hallway of the BRIDE's *house. The front door is at the rear. Nighttime. The* BRIDE *appears wearing a white petticoat, heavy with lace and embroidery, and a white bodice. Her arms are bare. The* MAID *is similarly dressed.*

MAID   I'll finish your hair here.

BRIDE   It's so hot inside.

MAID   In these parts there's not even a breath of cool air at dawn.

The BRIDE *sits on a low chair and looks at herself in a small hand-mirror. The* MAID *combs her hair.*

BRIDE   My mother came from a place full of trees . . . from rich land.

MAID   She was so full of life!

BRIDE   And she withered away here.

MAID   That was her fate.[24]

BRIDE   As we all slowly wither. Even the walls are burning . . . Oh, don't pull so hard.

MAID   I want to get this wave just right. So that it falls over your forehead.   *The* BRIDE *looks at herself in the mirror.*   You're so lovely. Ay!   *She kisses her impulsively.*

BRIDE   *serious*   Finish my hair.

MAID   *combing her hair*   You're so lucky . . . to hug a man, to kiss him . . . to feel his weight on top of you . . .

BRIDE   Be quiet.

MAID   And the best bit is when you wake up, and you feel him beside you, his breath tickling your shoulders, like a nightingale's feather . . .[25]

BRIDE *fiercely* Just shut up!

MAID But, my love, that's what a wedding's all about. There's much more to it than this, than just sweets and flowers. Oh yes . . . it's a shining bed . . . and a man and a woman.

BRIDE You've no business talking about such things.

MAID Perhaps not. But it's the real joy of it.

BRIDE Or the real bitterness.

MAID I'm going to fix the orange blossom right across here, so that it sets off your hair. Like this. *She holds the orange blossom against her hair.*

BRIDE *looking at herself in the mirror* Give it to me. *She takes the orange blossom, looks at it and drops her head disconsolately.*

MAID What's all this?

BRIDE Just leave me in peace.

MAID This is no time for heartaches. *Encouragingly.* Give me the orange blossom. *The* BRIDE *throws it to the floor.* Child! Throwing away your wedding wreath – you're asking for trouble, you're tempting fate. Look at me . . . do you not want to get married? Speak now . . . it's still not too late. *She stands up.*

BRIDE It's like clouds in my mind . . . or as though I'd suddenly been caught in a chill wind. It's normal . . .

MAID Do you love him?

BRIDE I love him.

MAID I know you do.

BRIDE But it's such a big step.

MAID You'll have to take it sometime.

BRIDE   I've said I will.

MAID   I'll fix your wedding wreath for you.

BRIDE   *sitting down*   Hurry up. They'll be here soon.

MAID   They've been on the road for a couple of hours already.

BRIDE   How long is it from here to the church?

MAID   Two hours by the river, twice as much if you go by the path.

The BRIDE *stands up and the* MAID *watches her admiringly.*

MAID
Let the bride awaken
on her wedding morn.
Across a thousand rivers
her wedding wreath is borne.

BRIDE   *smiling*
Come on.

MAID   *kissing her warmly and dancing around her*
Let the bride awaken
under the ripe green bough
of the sweet laurel flower.
Let the bride awaken
with the stem and bough
of the rich white laurel flower.

A loud knock is heard.

BRIDE   Go and see who it is. It must be the first guests.   *She goes inside.*

The MAID *opens in surprise.*

MAID   Oh, it's you.

LEONARDO   Yes. Good morning.

MAID   You're the first.

LEONARDO   Wasn't I invited?

MAID   Of course.

LEONARDO   Well, here I am.

MAID   What about your wife?

LEONARDO   I came by horse . . . she's coming the long
way round.

MAID   And you didn't see anybody else on the way?

LEONARDO   I rode past them.

MAID   You're running that poor beast into the ground.

LEONARDO   When I do, that's where he can stay.

    Pause.

MAID   Sit down. Nobody's up yet.

LEONARDO   Not even the bride?

MAID   I'm going in to dress her now.

LEONARDO   The bride! Her big day![26]

MAID   *changing the subject*   What about the baby?

LEONARDO   Whose baby?

MAID   Your baby!

LEONARDO   *remembering, as though in a dream*   Ah!

MAID   Are they bringing him?

LEONARDO   No.

    Pause. Distant singing.

VOICES
    Let the bride awaken
    on her wedding morn.[27]

LEONARDO
    Let the bride awaken
    on her wedding morn.

MAID   That's them now. But they've still got a good
        way to come.

LEONARDO   *standing up*   She'll wear a large wedding
        wreath, won't she? Not too big . . . a smaller one
        would suit her better. Has the bridegroom brought
        the orange blossom yet . . . for her breast?

BRIDE   *appearing in her petticoat, and wearing the orange
        blossom*   Yes, he has.

MAID   *emphatically*   You mustn't come out like that!

BRIDE   Why shouldn't I? *Seriously.*   Why do you ask?
        Have you got something to say about it?

LEONARDO   Nothing. Why should I have? *Moving
        closer to her.*   You know me, you know I haven't.
        But you tell me something . . . What did I really
        mean to you? Try and think, cast your mind back
        . . . A pair of oxen and a tumbledown shack were
        never enough for you, were they? That's the real
        hurt of it.

BRIDE   What are you doing here like this?

LEONARDO   I'm here to see you married.

BRIDE   Just as I saw you married.

LEONARDO   What choice did I have? My hands had been
        tied a long time back. You can take a knife or gun to
        me, but nobody will spit at me, no matter how
        much shining silver they have.

BRIDE   That's not true.

LEONARDO   Look, I'm not going to talk about this any
        more because I can feel my blood starting to boil,
        and I don't want the whole countryside to hear what
        I've got to say.[28]

BRIDE   I can shout every bit as much as you.

MAID   Neither of you will say anything. What's done is

59

done and what's lost is lost . . . and gone for
ever.   *She looks at the door, increasingly anxious.*

BRIDE   You're right. I shouldn't even be speaking to
you. But the way you've come here today, to spy
on me at my own wedding, raking through things
long past, fills me full of rage . . . Go and wait for
your wife . . . outside.

LEONARDO   Can we not even speak together?

MAID   *angrily*   No. You can't.

LEONARDO   Yes . . . I got married, and ever since then,
day and night, I've asked myself whose fault it was,
and each time I find somebody else to blame . . .
because there's always blame.

BRIDE   Oh, yes, you're so strong, so clever, you ride
your horse so well . . . and I'm just a poor girl
stuck out here in the desert. But I've got my pride
too. And that's why I'm getting married. I'll lock
myself away with my husband, and love him above
all other things, and I'll do right by him.

LEONARDO   You can't hide behind your pride.   *He
draws nearer.*

BRIDE   Stay away from me!

LEONARDO   To burn in silence is the worst punishment
we can inflict upon ourselves. What good did pride
do me – what use was it pretending you didn't exist,
leaving you to lie awake night in, night out? None
. . . none at all. I burned all the more. Because you
think things like that fade with time or that they can
be locked away behind thick walls. And they can't.
They can't. And when they reach their centre,
they're unstoppable, like water rising in a deep
well.[29]

BRIDE   *trembling*   I won't listen to you . . . I daren't
listen to your voice. It's as though I'd drunk a bottle

of sweet wine and I was lying on a bed of flowers.
And I feel myself being dragged along and I know
I'm drowning, but I go anyway.[30]

MAID   *grabbing* LEONARDO *by the lapels*   Go! Now!

LEONARDO   This is the last time I'll ever speak to her.
You needn't worry.

BRIDE   I know I'm crazy, and I know he's tearing my
heart, and yet here I am quietly, meekly listening to
him, watching him strutting round my room . . .

LEONARDO   I won't rest until I've said this: I got
married. Now you must.

MAID   *to* LEONARDO   She's going to! And don't you
forget it.

VOICES   *singing, closer*
Let the bride awaken
on her wedding morn.

BRIDE   Dear God, let the bride awaken!   *She runs off to
her room.*[31]

MAID   That's the first of the guests now.   *To*
LEONARDO.   You stay away from her.

LEONARDO   Don't worry.   *He exits stage left.*

Day is beginning to break.

GIRL 1   *entering*
Let the bride awaken
on her wedding day,
the wheel of life goes round
her wedding wreath today.[32]

VOICES
The bride! The bride!

MAID   *animatedly*
Let the bride awaken
under the sweet green bough

of love in flower.
Let the bride awaken
with the stem and bough
of the white laurel flower.

GIRL 2   *entering*
Let the bride awaken
and slowly begin to stir,
her blouse of shining snow,
jasmines through her hair.

MAID
The bride! The bride!
Before the moon has gone.

GIRL 1
The bride! The bride!
Before her love has flown.

BOY 1   *entering, holding his hat in the air*
Let the bride awaken
her wedding fills the air,
the scent of roses,
the aroma of bread,
life's kiss everywhere.

VOICES
The bride! The bride!

GIRL 2
The bride comes
with her silver flowing train,
the bridegroom winds her round his heart
with a flowing golden chain.

MAID
In the lemon grove
lies the bride of love.

GIRL 3   *entering*
In the orange grove
the bridegroom lays her down.

Three GUESTS *enter.*

BOY 1

> On her wedding day
> the bride arises
> as gentle as any dove.
> The dawn bell chimes,
> chasing night with love.

GUEST

> The bride, the white, white bride,
> the warm day awaits
> before your night of love.

GIRL 1

> Come down now to us,
> little dark-eyed one
> with your long train of silk,
> your shining smile of sun.

GUEST

> Come down now to us
> with your jet black hair,
> throw your balcony open
> to the brightening air.

BOY 1

> Arise, young bride, arise
> orange blossoms fill the skies.

MAID

> I would weave for you
> a splendid tree alive,
> decked with purple ribbons
> of love and cries of joy.

VOICES

> The bride! The bride!

BOY 1

> Your wedding day has come!

GUEST
Your wedding day at last
when you'll be crowned with love
as fair as any flower,
as pure as any dove.

FATHER   *entering*
Fair and pure indeed,
my only treasure, my only joy,
to the bridegroom I give today.

GIRL 3
The bridegroom, the bridegroom,
the golden flower of the sun,
the silver dagger of the moon.

MAID
My little one,
how happy you'll be today.

BOY 2
The bride! The bride!

MAID
And happier yet
when the night draws close
and the light has gone away.

GIRL 1
Your wedding is calling
and calling
through the rising air.

GIRL 2
The bride! The bride!

GIRL 1
The bride! The bride!

MAID
Let the bells ring
and ring again.

BOY 1
>   Here she comes.
>   She's coming now.

MAID
>   With the power of a bull
>   the wedding begins.

The BRIDE appears. She is wearing a black dress, in the style of the early 1900s, very tight around her hips, and with a train of gauze and lace. On her head, the orange blossom crown. The sound of guitars. The GIRLS come to embrace the BRIDE.

GIRL 3   What scent have you got on your hair?

BRIDE   *laughing*   None at all.

GIRL 3   *looking at the dress*   Your dress is out of this world.

BOY 1   Here's the groom!

BRIDEGROOM   Good health to everyone!

GIRL 1   *placing a flower behind his ear*
>   The bridegroom, the bridegroom
>   the golden flower of the sun.

GIRL 2
>   The bridegroom, the bridegroom
>   the silver dagger of the moon.

The BRIDEGROOM goes over to the BRIDE.

BRIDE   What made you wear those shoes?

BRIDEGROOM   They're brighter than my black ones.

WIFE   *entering and kissing the BRIDE*   I wish you both every joy.

They talk together animatedly.

LEONARDO *entering as one performing a duty*
This day you'll be wed
the wedding wreath
we place upon your head.

WIFE
So that life from you will flow
like the sun to brighten the land
with its glow.

MOTHER *to the* FATHER   What are they doing here?

FATHER   They're family. Today we forgive.

MOTHER   I'll say nothing . . . but I won't forgive.

BRIDEGROOM   The orange blossom has brought the sun
to your hair.

BRIDE   Let's get to the church as quickly as we can.

BRIDEGROOM   You can't wait to get married?

BRIDE   No. All I want is to be your wife and to be alone
with you, and to shut out everyone's voice but
yours.

BRIDEGROOM   Just the two of us . . .

BRIDE   And to fix my eyes on yours. And for you to
hold me so tight that even if my dead mother called
me I couldn't break free . . .

BRIDEGROOM   My arms are strong enough to hug and
hold you for forty years without letting go.

BRIDE   *dramatically, taking his arm*   Don't let me go . . .
ever.

FATHER   We must get a move on. Get the coaches and
the carts . . . the sun's already up.

MOTHER   Go easy . . . let's not start the day badly.

The large door at the back opens. They begin to leave.

MAID *crying*
> You leave your house
> a girl so white
> your body like a star
> shining to the night

GIRL 1
> A girl white and fair
> you fly from your house
> like a star through the air.

> *They leave.*

GIRL 2
> Here comes the bride!

MAID
> The breeze carries flowers
> through the air.

GIRL 3
> The beautiful bride!

MAID
> The breeze gently
> lifts the lace from her hair.

> *They leave. Rhythmical music of guitars and
> tambourines. LEONARDO and his WIFE are left alone.*

WIFE   Shall we go?

LEONARDO   Where?

WIFE   The church. But not by horse. You're coming
with me.

LEONARDO   In the cart?

WIFE   Have you any other suggestion?

LEONARDO   I have no intention of climbing into any
cart.

WIFE   And I have no intention of going to a wedding

without my husband. I can't take much more of this.

LEONARDO   That makes two of us.

WIFE   Why do you look at me like that? As though you had a dagger in each eye.

LEONARDO   Let's just go.

WIFE   I don't understand . . . I think and I don't want to think. But one thing I do know . . . it's over . . . and I have a child and another on the way. And you say let's go . . . the same thing that happened to my poor mother is happening to me. I'm not moving from here . . .

Voices are heard outside.

VOICES
A girl white and fair
you fly from your house
like a star through the air.

WIFE   *weeping*
You fly from your house
like a star through the air.
I flew so happily from mine as well . . . with the whole world in my heart and mouth.

LEONARDO   *standing up*   Let's go.

WIFE   The two of us!

LEONARDO   Yes. *Pause.* Come on. *They leave.*

VOICES
A girl white and fair
you fly from your house
like a star through the air.

Slow Curtain.

Outside the BRIDE's *home. Tones of greyish white and cold blue. The whole atmosphere is sombre and silvery. Large cacti. In the background brownish hills in sharp relief, as though painted on ceramics.*

MAID   *arranging glasses and trays on a table*
The wheel was turning, turning
as the water was flowing, flowing
all on the wedding day,
and through dark branches
the moon is watching, watching
over the bride's white balcony.

In a loud voice.

Get those tablecloths pressed!

In a voice full of pathos.

And the lovers were singing, singing
as the water was flowing, flowing
all on the wedding day
and on white frost
the sun is shining, shining
pouring down like thick honey.

In a loud voice.

Get the wine poured!

In a voice full of poetry.

Young maid,
young maid of earth and fire,
watch how the water flows,
and on this your wedding day
pick up your skirts
and under your husband's wing
dwell in his house for ever.
For he is the dove

with a burning heart of flame,
and the fields await the murmur
of the spilling of your blood.
And the wheel was turning, turning
as the water was flowing, flowing.
All on your wedding day,
young maid,
make the water glow.[33]

MOTHER *entering* At long last!

FATHER Are we the first back?

MAID No. Leonardo and his wife arrived a good while
ago. He drove back like a man possessed. His wife
was scared out of her wits. You'd have thought he
was riding a horse rather than driving a cart.

FATHER He'll come to a sticky end that one . . . bad
blood, bad blood.

MOTHER What do you expect but bad blood? His
whole family's rotten with it, ever since his
grandfather . . . he was the first of the murdering
line, and they've all taken after him, with their
knives and cold smiles.

FATHER Let's forget it.

MAID How can she just forget it?

MOTHER Even the blood flowing in my veins seems to
ache. And when I look into their eyes . . . all I can
see is the hand that struck down my husband and
son . . . You think I'm crazy, don't you? Well, if I
am it's because I've locked too much away. But I'm
screaming inside all the time, because I know who
should be punished, and I know who really deserves
the shroud. And they just come and they take your
dead away, and you've got to stop screaming. And
then the gossips start. *She takes off her shawl.*

FATHER Today of all days . . .

MOTHER   What else can I do when I see one of them?
          And today of all days . . . Because from now on I'll
          be alone in my house.

FATHER   Perhaps not for long.

MOTHER   It's the only thought which keeps me going:
          my grandchildren.   *They sit down.*

FATHER   I hope they have a houseful of them. This land
          needs willing workers, cheap labour . . . so that
          they can fight against the weeds, the thistles and the
          rocks which just seem to spring from nowhere. It's
          got to be the men who own the land who punish it
          and tame it, who bring life from it. Yes, they'll need
          a lot of sons.

MOTHER   And daughters. Men come and go like the
          wind. They've got to carry knives and guns. But
          girls never even need to set foot in the street.

FATHER   *happily*   I'm sure they'll have a good few of
          each.

MOTHER   My son will cover her well. He's from good
          stock. His father would have had lots of children
          with me . . .

FATHER   I just wish they could get the whole business
          over in a single day. That they could have two or
          three grown men straightaway.

MOTHER   That's not the way of things. It's a long
          painful process. Which is why it's so terrible to see
          your own blood spilt in the dust . . . a fountain of
          blood that spurts for just a single minute, and which
          has taken years out of your life. When I got to my
          son, he was lying in the middle of the street, and I
          soaked my hands in his blood, and licked them with
          my tongue. Because it was mine as well. Can you
          understand that? And if I could I would take that
          dust red with his blood and put it into a crystal
          cup.[34]

FATHER   It's just a question of time now. My daughter is broad–hipped and your son is strong.

MOTHER   Yes, I know.   *They stand up*.

FATHER   Get the food and drink ready.

MAID   They are ready.

WIFE   *entering*   I hope they'll both be very happy.

MOTHER   Thank you.

LEONARDO   Are you planning a big celebration?

FATHER   Not really. Nobody can stay very long.

MAID   Here they come now.

> *Small groups of* GUESTS *enter merrily. The* BRIDE *and* BRIDEGROOM *enter arm in arm.* LEONARDO *leaves.*[35]

BRIDEGROOM   Have you ever seen such a wedding?

BRIDE   *serious*   Never.

FATHER   It was splendid.

MOTHER   There are whole families here.

BRIDEGROOM   People who hardly ever set foot across their own doorway.

MOTHER   You're reaping what your father sowed.

BRIDEGROOM   There are cousins of mine here that I've never even met before.

MOTHER   All the ones from the coast . . .

BRIDEGROOM   *cheerfully*   They were a bit wary of the horses.

> *They talk*.

MOTHER   *to the* BRIDE   What are you thinking?

BRIDE   Nothing in particular.

MOTHER   So many good wishes . . . they can weigh heavy.

Guitars are heard.

BRIDE   Like lead.

MOTHER   *energetically*   But you mustn't let them. You should feel as light as a dove.

BRIDE   Will you stay here with us tonight?

MOTHER   I can't. My house is empty.

BRIDE   You should stay.

FATHER   *to the* MOTHER   Look at them dancing, your people from the coast. Rising and falling like the waves of the sea.[36]

LEONARDO *appears and sits down. His* WIFE *stands behind him, tense.*

MOTHER   My husband's cousins. As strong as trees, they could dance for ever.

FATHER   They're a sight for sore eyes in this house. *He leaves.*

BRIDEGROOM   *to the* BRIDE   Did you like the orange blossom?

BRIDE   *staring straight at him*   Yes.

BRIDEGROOM   It's real wax, you know. It'll never fade or wither. I'd have liked to cover your whole dress with it.

BRIDE   There was no need to.

LEONARDO *exits silently from the right.*

GIRL 1   Shall we help you take the pins from your veil?

BRIDE   *to the* BRIDEGROOM   I won't be long.

WIFE   I hope you'll be happy with my cousin.

BRIDEGROOM   I'm sure I will be.

WIFE   Just the two of you here, building your house together and then closing out the world. If only we had somewhere like this.

BRIDEGROOM   You could always invest in some land. It's cheap over towards the mountains, and it's better for the children.

WIFE   We haven't got any money. And with the way things are going . . .

BRIDEGROOM   Your husband is a good worker.

WIFE   Perhaps, but he won't settle to anything. Always flitting from one thing to the next. He never seems at peace.

MAID   You're not eating! I'll go and get some wine-cakes for your mother, she adores them.

BRIDEGROOM   Get her a couple of dozen.

WIFE   No, no. Just a few.

BRIDEGROOM   No. This is a special day.

WIFE   *to the* MAID   Have you seen my Leonardo?

MAID   No, I'm sorry.

BRIDEGROOM   He must be out there with the rest of them.

WIFE   I'll go and look for him.   *She leaves.*

MAID   Isn't it gorgeous?

BRIDEGROOM   How come you're not dancing?

MAID   Perhaps because nobody's asked me.

> *Two* GIRLS *cross over at the back. During this whole scene there is a constant coming and going of wedding guests.*

BRIDEGROOM *cheerfully* Because they don't know any better. A lively one like you could teach a thing or two to any of these youngsters.

MAID Ah, so you're starting to come the young gallant with me now, are you? You're your father's son all right. A man among men. When I was just a tiny thing I saw your grandfather's wedding. I remember well the cut of him. Like a mountain coming down the aisle.

BRIDEGROOM I haven't quite got the same build.

MAID But you've got the same gleam in your eye. Where's the little one?

BRIDEGROOM Taking off her veil.

MAID Ah! Listen. I'm sure that neither of you will be exactly fast asleep at midnight, so I've cut some ham and left it, along with a couple of glasses of good wine, in the bottom part of the larder. Just in case.

BRIDEGROOM *smiling* I never eat at night.

MAID *maliciously* Perhaps not . . . but I'm sure the bride's appetite will have been . . . well whetted by then. *She leaves.*

BOY 1 *entering* Come and have a drink with us.

BRIDEGROOM I'm waiting for . . . my wife.[37]

BOY 2 You'll have her soon enough.

BOY 1 Just before dawn, that's the best time.

BOY 2 Come on. Get a drink into you.

BRIDEGROOM All right.

They leave. An atmosphere of great animation. The
BRIDE *appears, and two* GIRLS *run over to meet her.*

GIRL 1 Who did you give the first pin to? Her or me?

BRIDE   I'm really not sure . . .

GIRL 1   You gave it to me . . . here.

GIRL 2   No, you gave it to me . . . in front of the altar.

BRIDE   *tense, as though a great battle were raging inside her*   I don't know.

GIRL 1   It's just that I'd like you to . . .

BRIDE   *interrupting her*   Look, I've got enough to think about without . . .

GIRL 2   Sorry.

LEONARDO *crosses in the background.*

BRIDE   *catching sight of* LEONARDO   I've got a lot on my mind.

GIRL 1   We wouldn't know anything about that . . .

BRIDE   You'll know soon enough. Getting married is a big thing, you know . . .[38]

GIRL 1   You seem upset.

BRIDE   No, of course I'm not. I'm sorry.

GIRL 2   What for? Anyway both pins mean you'll get married, don't they?

BRIDE   Both of them, yes.

GIRL 1   But the thing is that whoever gets the first one gets married first.

BRIDE   And you're both in so much of a hurry?

GIRL 2   *embarrassedly*   Well, yes . . .

BRIDE   But why?

GIRL 1   Can't you guess?   *Hugging her friend.*

Both run off. The BRIDEGROOM *appears slowly, and quietly embraces the* BRIDE *from behind.*

BRIDE *startled* Stop it!

BRIDEGROOM Did I frighten you?

BRIDE Oh, it's you.

BRIDEGROOM Who else would it be? *Pause.* Your father or me.

BRIDE I know.

BRIDEGROOM Except your father would have been gentler.

BRIDE *serious* Of course.

BRIDEGROOM Because he's an old man. *He embraces her tightly, roughly.*

BRIDE *sharply* Not now.

BRIDEGROOM Why not? *Releasing her.*

BRIDE Because . . . somebody might see us.

The MAID crosses over, studiously ignoring the couple.

BRIDEGROOM So what? We've got the church's blessing, you know.

BRIDE Perhaps, but not now . . . Later on.

BRIDEGROOM What's wrong with you? You seem nervous.

BRIDE Nothing's wrong. Don't go.

LEONARDO's WIFE appears.

WIFE I don't mean to interrupt . . .

BRIDEGROOM What is it?

WIFE You haven't seen my husband, have you?

BRIDEGROOM No.

WIFE He doesn't seem to be anywhere . . . his horse has gone too.

BRIDEGROOM *cheerfully* He'll have taken it out for a run.

The WIFE *leaves anxiously. The* MAID *enters.*

MAID You must be both feeling on top of the world . . . all this big fuss just for you, eh?

BRIDEGROOM I'm starting to get a bit sick of it all. She's feeling a bit tense.

MAID What's the matter, sweetheart?

BRIDE My head's pounding.

MAID A bride from these parts has to be stronger than that . . . *To the* BRIDEGROOM. You're the only one who can do anything with her now . . . she belongs to you. *She leaves quickly.*

BRIDEGROOM *embracing her* Let's go and dance. *He kisses her.*

BRIDE *very tense* No. I want to lie down for a while.

BRIDEGROOM I'll keep you company . . .

BRIDE No! With everyone still here . . . what on earth would they all say? Just give me five minutes.

BRIDEGROOM All right . . . but when they've gone . . .

BRIDE *from the doorway* I'll be all right by then.

BRIDEGROOM Make sure you are . . .

The MOTHER *enters.*

MOTHER Son.

BRIDEGROOM Where have you been?

MOTHER Just wandering through the crowd. Are you happy?

BRIDEGROOM Yes.

MOTHER And the bride?

BRIDEGROOM   She's having a rest. A bad day for brides!

MOTHER   Bad? It's the very best of days. It was the opening up of a new world for me.   *The* MAID *comes in and goes to the* BRIDE's *room.*   It's the earth turning and seeds growing . . .[39]

BRIDEGROOM   Stay here tonight.

MOTHER   I can't. I must get home.

BRIDEGROOM   Just to sit on your own?

MOTHER   How will I be on my own? My head is full of memories of my men and the fights they fought.

BRIDEGROOM   But that's all those fights are now . . . memories.

The MAID *reappears and hurries across the stage.*

MOTHER   I'll fight on for as long as I live.

BRIDEGROOM   Whatever you say.

MOTHER   Listen . . ., always be affectionate with your wife, but if you think she's getting too starry-eyed or too sour, then caress her just so that it hurts . . . a bruising hug or a bite, and then a gentle kiss. She won't take it amiss, and she'll know exactly who's who, who gives the orders and who takes them. That's how your father taught me. And now that he's gone, it's up to me to teach you.[40]

BRIDEGROOM   I'll always do whatever you tell me.

FATHER   *entering*   Have you seen my daughter?

BRIDEGROOM   She went inside.

GIRL 1   We want the bride and groom . . . everyone's going to dance in a ring.

BOY 1   *to the* BRIDEGROOM   With you in the middle.

FATHER   *appearing*   She's not there.

BRIDEGROOM   Isn't she?

FATHER   She must have gone up to the balcony.

BRIDEGROOM   I'll run up and look.   *He goes off.*

Sound of singing and guitars.

GIRL 1   They've started without us.   *She leaves.*

BRIDEGROOM   *returning*   She's not there.

MOTHER   *worriedly*   No?

FATHER   Where can she have got to?

MAID   *coming in*   Has anyone seen . . .?

MOTHER   *sombre*   No.

The BRIDEGROOM *leaves. Three* GUESTS *come in.*

FATHER   *dramatically*   You're sure she's not dancing?

MAID   She's not dancing.

FATHER   *his nerves exploding*   The place is packed! Go and look!

MAID   I have looked.

FATHER   *tragically*   Well, where is she?

BRIDEGROOM   *returning*   No sign of her . . . nowhere.

MOTHER   *to the* FATHER   Just what's going on here? Where is your daughter?

LEONARDO'S WIFE *comes in.*

WIFE   They've gone . . . together. Leonardo and her. On his horse . . . I've just seen them . . . riding like the wind, hugged tightly together.[41]

FATHER   God help us, no . . . not my daughter.

MOTHER   Oh yes, yes! Yes, your daughter. Her mother's daughter. And he's as bad as the rest of his family. I warned you. But she's my son's wife now.

BRIDEGROOM   Let's go after them. Somebody get a
horse.

MOTHER   Get a horse quickly! Someone . . . anyone. I'll
buy it with everything that's mine, with my tongue
and eyes if need be.

VOICE   There's one here.

MOTHER   *to the* BRIDEGROOM   Go on! Go!   *He makes
to leave, accompanied by two* GUESTS.   Oh, but no . . .
those people are so quick to kill. But what else can
you do? You have to go, and me with you.

FATHER   It can't have been her! She would have thrown
herself down the well first.

MOTHER   If she'd any shame that's what she would have
done. But there's not a drop of decency in her. And
she's my son's wife now. You remember that!
There are two families here. Yours and mine. We'll
go after her . . . and we'll help my son. And we'll
shake the dust of this place from our feet.   *The
crowd splits into two groups.*   Because he's got
family; people who count; his cousins from the
coast, and all the men who've come to this wedding
from miles around. Let's go . . . some of you by the
river, others over the plain, and the rest through the
hills and forest. And I tell you this . . . blood will
flow before this day is over. Two families. You and
yours, me and mine. Let's go! Now!

Curtain.

A forest. Night. Large moist tree trunks. An atmosphere of darkness. Two violins are heard. Three WOODCUTTERS *appear.*[42]

WOODCUTTER 1   Have they found them yet?

WOODCUTTER 2   Not yet. But they'll not leave a single stone unturned.

WOODCUTTER 3   They'll get them.

WOODCUTTER 2   Ssssh!

WOODCUTTER 3   What?

WOODCUTTER 2   They're closing round . . . along every path.

WOODCUTTER 1   They'll see them as soon as the moon rises.

WOODCUTTER 2   They should let them go.

WOODCUTTER 1   The world is wide. There's room for everyone.

WOODCUTTER 3   But they'll kill them.

WOODCUTTER 2   They were right to run away . . . to take their own path.

WOODCUTTER 1   They were just fooling themselves, until at last their blood began to simmer . . .

WOODCUTTER 3   Blood.

WOODCUTTER 1   And they followed the pulse of their blood. What else could they do?

WOODCUTTER 2   Blood that sees the light of day is quickly buried in earth.

WOODCUTTER 1   What of it? Better to die of bloodletting than to live with it stagnant in your veins.

WOODCUTTER 3   Be still . . .

WOODCUTTER 1   What? What do you hear?

WOODCUTTER 3   The cicadas, the frogs . . . and the
sprung trap of night.

WOODCUTTER 1   But not the horse.

WOODCUTTER 3   No. Not the horse.

WOODCUTTER 1   Then he's with her now.

WOODCUTTER 2   His body for her . . . and hers for
him.[43]

WOODCUTTER 3   They'll find them and kill them.

WOODCUTTER 1   But by then their blood will be one,
and they'll be like two empty pitchers, two streams
run dry.

WOODCUTTER 2   The night is heavy, perhaps the moon
won't rise.

WOODCUTTER 3   With or without the moon, the
bridegroom will find them. I watched him rush
from the wedding. Like a raging star. His face the
colour of ash. Carrying the weight of his father and
brother upon his shoulders.

WOODCUTTER 1   The weight of his whole family lying
dead in the street.

WOODCUTTER 2   Lying dead.

WOODCUTTER 3   Do you think they'll break the circle?

WOODCUTTER 2   Impossible. There are knives and guns
for ten miles around.

WOODCUTTER 3   He has a good horse.

WOODCUTTER 2   But there are two of them now . . .

WOODCUTTER 1   This is the tree.

WOODCUTTER 2   Forty branches high. We'll soon bring
it down.

WOODCUTTER 3   The moon's rising. We'll have to
hurry.[44]

A brilliant light begins to rise on the left.

WOODCUTTER 1
The moon
rising over the wood.

WOODCUTTER 2
Cover their red blood
with white flowers.

WOODCUTTER 1
The lonely, lonely moon
moon on the green leaves.

WOODCUTTER 2
Silver on the bride's face.

WOODCUTTER 3
Evil, evil moon
leave the world to darkness
and to love.

WOODCUTTER 1
Sad, sad moon
leave the world to darkness
and to love

*They leave. The MOON appears, surrounded by brilliant
light. A young WOODCUTTER with a white face. The
scene acquires a brilliant blue glow.*

MOON
Round swan in the river,
the cathedral's eye,
false dawn on the leaves;
all these things am I; they won't escape!
Who can hide? Who's that sobbing there

in the valley thicket,
on the dark mountainside?
The moon leaves a knife hanging in the sky,
a cold trap of lead
that seeks blood's warm cry.
Let me in! I come frozen and numbed
through walls and glass!
Open your homes and breasts
so that I can warm myself.
I'm freezing. I seek the crest of fire
through streets and mountains
to warm my body of ashes
and brooding metals.
But instead
I ride the dark night
and across water and snow
as cold as the dead
I am made to go.
But this night
red, red blood will caress
my blue cheeks
in the hush of reeds
over the broad steps of the air.
Let there be no shadow or shade
where they can hide.
Tonight, I want
a heart split wide
so that I may warm myself.
A human heart for me!
Warm, draining itself
over the the mountains of my breast.
Let me in, oh let me in.

To the branches.

I'll have no shadow. My rays
must be everywhere
filling the dark trees
with the murmur of false day

so that tonight
my cheeks will feel the caress
of sweet red blood,
in the hush of reeds
over the broad steps of the air.
Who's that hiding there?
There's no way out for you.
I'll make the horse gleam
with a diamond's fever. [45]

The MOON *disappears amongst the branches, and the scene
returns to darkness. A* BEGGARWOMAN *appears, dressed
in dark-green rags. She is barefooted, her face hidden
between the folds of her cloak. This character does not
appear in the cast list.*

BEGGAR
The moon has gone, and they're close by.
They'll go no further. Here the dark music
of the forest will still their cry.
It must be here, and soon. I'm tired.
White sheets across empty bedroom floors
grow impatient for the return
of heavy bodies with their throats cut.
Not a single bird will stir
and the breeze will sweep their screams
through the black tree tops
to bury them after in dark wet earth.

Impatient.

The moon . . . where's the moon?

The MOON *emerges. The intense light returns.*

MOON
They're drawing close.
Some by the river, others through the mountain
pass. I'll drown them in light. What else
do you need?

BEGGAR

Nothing.

MOON

Watch how the air hardens
how its profile sharpens.

BEGGAR

Just make their waistcoat buttons gleam
after that, the knives like fish
will come marauding in . . .[46]

MOON

But let them be slow in the dying. I want
their blood to fill my fingers
with its delicate whisper. Already I can feel
the ashen dust of my valleys stir
in expectation of its rich fountain,
its shivering spurt.

BEGGAR

We won't let them go beyond the stream. Now
silence!

MOON

They're coming now.

The MOON *leaves. The scene is left in darkness.*

BEGGAR   Quickly! Light . . . light everywhere. Do you
hear? They mustn't escape

The BRIDEGROOM *and* BOY 1 *appear. The*
BEGGARWOMAN *sits down and covers herself with her
cloak.*

BRIDEGROOM   This way.

BOY   You'll never find them.

BRIDEGROOM   *fiercely*   I'll find them.

BOY   They'll have gone another way.

BRIDEGROOM   No. I heard the drumming of hooves a moment ago.

BOY   It might have been a different horse.

BRIDEGROOM   *dramatically*   Listen. In the whole wide world there's only one horse, just one. Do you understand? If you're going to follow me, follow me in silence.

BOY   I just meant . . .

BRIDEGROOM   Shut up! I know I'll find them here. There's a strength in my arm flowing from my brother and father, from all my family's dead, so that if I had to I could rip this tree up by the roots. Now, let's get going, because I feel as if their teeth had bitten right into my heart, so that I can hardly breathe.

BEGGAR   *moaning*   Ay!

BOY   What was that?

BRIDEGROOM   Go through there . . . and work your way back.

BOY   This is like hunting for a needle in a haystack.

BRIDEGROOM   A hunt. The most terrible you can imagine.

The BOY *leaves. The* BRIDEGROOM *goes rapidly towards the left, and stumbles over the* BEGGARWOMAN.

BEGGAR   Ay!

BRIDEGROOM   Who are you? What do you want?

BEGGAR   I'm cold.

BRIDEGROOM   Where are you going?

BEGGAR   *in a whining voice*   Far, far from here.

BRIDEGROOM   Where have you come from?

BEGGAR   From way, way back.

BRIDEGROOM   Have you seen a man and woman on
      horseback?

BEGGAR   *slowly stirring* Wait . . . *Looking at him.*
      Handsome young man.   *She stands up.*
      But handsomer still if he were asleep.

BRIDEGROOM   Answer me . . . did you see them?

BEGGAR   Not so fast . . . Such broad shoulders! So much
      easier to lie flat on them than to have to walk on feet
      which are so, so small.

BRIDEGROOM   *shaking her* I'm asking you if you saw
      them. Did they come this way or not?

BEGGAR   *energetically* Not this way . . . but they're
      coming out of the hills now. Can't you hear them?

BRIDEGROOM   No.

BEGGAR   You don't know the way?

BRIDEGROOM   I'll go anyhow.

BEGGAR   Then I'll take you. I know these parts well.

BRIDEGROOM   Let's go. Which way?

BEGGAR   *dramatically* Come with me!

      *They leave quickly. In the distance can be heard two
      violins, the sound of the forest. The* WOODCUTTERS
      *return, carrying their axes over their shoulders. They move
      slowly amongst the tree trunks.*

WOODCUTTER 1
      Death
      rising over the wood.

WOODCUTTER 2
      Stem the flow of blood.

WOODCUTTER 1
Lonely, lonely death
Voice of dried-up leaves.

WOODCUTTER 3
Let their wedding grow.

WOODCUTTER 2
Sad, sad death
let the branch of love grow green.

WOODCUTTER 1
Evil, evil death
let the branch of love grow green.

They leave as they speak. LEONARDO *and the* BRIDE
appear.

LEONARDO
Hush!

BRIDE
I'll go my own way now.
Leave me. I want you to go back.

LEONARDO
Be quiet, I said.

BRIDE
With your teeth,
with your hands, whichever way you can,
cut the metal chain you've placed
around my neck
and which dragged me from my father's house.
And if you won't kill me,
as you would crush a baby viper,
then put the knife into my hands,
these hands that took his orange blossom . . .
My head is full of grief
and fire, and my tongue
run through and through
with sharpest glass.[47]

LEONARDO

> There's no going back, so hush,
> because they're hunting us close by,
> and I won't leave you now.

BRIDE

> Then it'll be by force that I go.

LEONARDO

> How by force? Who was it led the way
> down the stairs?

BRIDE

> I did.

LEONARDO

> And who strapped new bridles
> round the horse's mane?

BRIDE

> I did. I know.

LEONARDO

> And whose hands buckled on my spurs?

BRIDE

> My hands . . . which are yours
> and which if they could,
> as I watch you now,
> would snap and silence for ever
> the blue murmur of your veins.
> I love you. I love you. But leave me alone.
> Because if I could kill you
> I would wrap you now
> in a violet edged shroud.
> My head is full of grief and fire.

LEONARDO

> My tongue is run through and through
> with sharpest glass.
> Because I wanted to forget
> and I put a wall of stone

between your house and mine.
It's true. You remember, don't you?
And when I saw you pass by
I cast sand in my eyes.
But my horse
always took me to your door.
And the silver pins of your wedding
turned my blood black
and my flesh soured
and grew thick with weeds.
It's not me who's to blame,
it's the earth itself,
it's the scent of your breasts
and of your hair.

BRIDE

This is madness. I'll take
neither bread nor bed from you,
and yet there's not a single moment of the day
that I don't long to be with you,
it's as if you pull me along, and I just go,
you turn my whole world round
and I follow you through the air
like a blade of grass.
I left behind a man who was my husband
and his whole brooding family
in the middle of our wedding.
And you'll be the one to suffer for it,
and I don't want that.
Now leave me. Go.
There's no one who'll help you.

LEONARDO

The birds are stirring in the trees,
dawn's about to break,
and night is slowly dying
on the hard edge of stone.
Let's just go from here, to some dark corner,
where we can lie together

and not care about the poisoned tongues
whispering all around.[48]

He embraces her tightly.

BRIDE
And I'll lie at your feet
watching over your dreams.
Naked, lying on the land,

Dramatically.

like a bitch in heat. Because
that's what I am. I look at you
and feel myself burn.

LEONARDO
When fire meets fire
a single tiny flame
can set a whole forest ablaze.
Let's go.

He draws her after him.

BRIDE
And just where will you take me?

LEONARDO
Somewhere, anywhere
the men hunting us cannot go,
and where I can look at you.

BRIDE   *sarcastically*
Oh yes, to trail me round from fair to fair
in all my shame
so that everyone can stare at me
with my wedding sheets
like flags in the wind.[49]

LEONARDO
If I thought like them
I'd leave you here right now.
But I'll go where you go.

And you too. Just one step. Come on.
Splinters of moonlight have pierced
my waist and your hips.

The whole scene is very intense, full of a great sensuality.

BRIDE
Did you hear that?

LEONARDO
They're here.

BRIDE
Then go quickly.
It's only right that I should die here
beside the stream
with thorns in my hair,
and only the leaves to mourn
a lost woman and virgin.

LEONARDO
Be quiet. They're coming closer.

BRIDE
Go now!

LEONARDO
Quiet, and they won't hear us.
You go first. Let's go.

The BRIDE *hesitates.*

BRIDE
Both of us together.

LEONARDO   *hugging her tightly*
Both of us.
If they want to separate us
they'll have to kill me first.

BRIDE
And me.

They embrace and leave. The MOON *appears very
slowly, bathing the scene in a brilliant blue light. The two
violins sound again. Suddenly two long screams are
heard, and the violins fall silent. With the second scream
the* BEGGARWOMAN *appears, her back to the audience.
She opens her cloak and stands in the centre of the stage
like an immense bird. The* MOON *stops. The curtain falls
in the midst of an absolute silence.*

A white room with archways and thick walls. White stairways on the left and right. At the back a large arch and white wall. The floor is also gleaming white. This simple room has the ponderous feeling of a church. There are no tones or shadows, not even enough to create a sense of perspective. Two GIRLS dressed in dark blue are winding a skein of red wool.[50]

GIRL 1

    Wool, wool
    what would you do?

GIRL 2

    Her jasmine dress
    and his crystal tie.
    They were born at four
    and they died at ten.
    Two strands of wool
    and a single chain,
    two leaves of laurel,
    one bitter pain.

GIRL 3   *singing*

    Did you go to the wedding?

GIRL 1

    No.

GIRL 3

    Neither did I.
    I wonder what happened
    in the vineyards,
    what happened
    in the olive groves,
    what happened
    that nobody came back.
    Did you go to the wedding?

GIRL 2
> We've said we didn't.

GIRL 3 *leaving*
> Neither did I.

GIRL 2
> Wool, wool
> what would you sing?

GIRL 1
> Of wounds of wax
> and of white myrtle pain,
> of mornings asleep
> and of nights awake.

GIRL 3 *from the doorway*
> The winding wool
> winds down the hill
> and over the mountains
> running, running all the way
> right through the night
> to the break of day.

> *She goes.*

GIRL 2
> Wool, wool
> what would you say?

GIRL 1
> Bathed in silence
> bathed in blood,
> I saw them both
> the lover and the bridegroom
> lying stiff
> on the still riverside.

> *She stops and gazes at the wool.*

GIRL 3 *appearing in the doorway*
> The winding wool
> comes winding home.

Two bodies return
flesh of ivory
and hair of earth.
I hear them coming now.

She goes. LEONARDO'*s* WIFE *and* MOTHER–IN–LAW
appear. Both are in despair.

GIRL 1   Are they coming yet?

MOTHER–IN–LAW   *bitterly*   We don't know.

GIRL 2   Tell us about the wedding.

GIRL 1   Yes, tell us.

MOTHER–IN–LAW   *sharply*   There's nothing to tell.

WIFE   I want to go back . . . I want to know.

MOTHER–IN–LAW   *forcefully*
You, to your house
quiet and alone in your house.
To weep and grow old
behind the closed door.
No more. Whether he's alive or dead.
We'll nail the windows down
and let the rains and black nights
fall around us.[51]

WIFE
But what can have happened?

MOTHER–IN–LAW
It makes no difference.
Hide your face behind the veil,
and remember your children are yours
and yours alone. And sign his pillow
with a cross of grey ash.

They leave.

BEGGAR   *from the doorway*   A crust of bread, my pretty
girls?

GIRL 3   Get away from here.

The GIRLS *huddle together.*

BEGGAR   But why?

GIRL 3   Because of your whingeing voice. Go away!

GIRL 1   Don't be so cheeky!

BEGGAR   I could ask for your eyes, if I wanted. A cloud of birds follows me; this one's for you.

GIRL 3   Just leave me alone.

GIRL 2   *to the* BEGGARWOMAN   Don't pay any attention to her.

GIRL 1   Did you come by the stream?

BEGGAR   I came by the stream.

GIRL 1   *timidly*   Do you mind if I ask . . .?

BEGGAR   Yes, I saw them; they'll be here soon; two torrents of water stilled by the rock, two men slung round a horse's neck. Dead, with the beautiful night in their eyes.   *With delectation.*   Dead, yes, dead.

GIRL 1   Shut up, old woman, shut up!

BEGGAR   Their eyes like crushed flowers, and their teeth like fistfuls of hardened snow. Both asleep, only the bride finally awake, her dress and her hair dyed deep in blood. They're bringing them back now, snug in blankets. That's all there is to it. The way it had to be. Dark earth on the golden flower of the sun.[52]

She leaves. The GIRLS *bow their heads and leave as though in a trance.*

GIRL 1
Dark earth.

GIRL 2
On the golden flower.

GIRL 3

> In the golden sun
> they're bringing the dead men back.
> Dark-haired the one
> and dark-haired the other,
> while the dark-feathered nightingale
> wheels and grieves
> under the flowering sun.

She leaves. The stage is left empty. The MOTHER *enters with a* NEIGHBOUR. *The* NEIGHBOUR *is weeping.*

MOTHER   Stop your crying.

NEIGHBOUR   I can't.

MOTHER   Stop it, I said. *In the doorway.* Is there nobody here? *She raises her hands to her face.* My son should have been here. But now he's no more than a handful of flowers, just a voice growing dark behind the mountains. *Angrily, to the* NEIGHBOUR. Be quiet. I'll have no tears in my house. Because yours are tears from the eyes, nothing else. Mine will come when I'm alone, from the soles of my feet, from my roots, and they'll flow hotter than blood.[53]

NEIGHBOUR   Come home with me; you can't stay here.

MOTHER   I want to be here. In peace and quiet. They're all dead now. But I'll sleep easy tonight, free from the fear of guns and knives. Tonight it'll be other women who lean out into the rain watching for their sons. But not me. I'll sleep . . . and my sleep will be like a cold marble dove carrying white flowers and frost to his grave. . . consecrated ground . . . consecrated! No, it's not consecrated; it's a bed of clay to hold them and rock them in the sky. *A* WOMAN *dressed in black enters and goes stage right, where she kneels down. To the* NEIGHBOUR. Take your hands from your face. The days

to come will be terrible days. And I don't want to
see anyone in my house. I'll be alone . . . with
the earth. With my grief . . . and these four walls.
Ay! Ay! *She sits down, overcome by grief.*

NEIGHBOUR   Don't torture yourself.

MOTHER   *smoothing her hair back with her hands*   Yes,
I've got to pull myself together. Because the
neighbours won't be long in coming, and I don't
want them to see me so poor. So, so poor. A
woman with not a single child to raise to her lips. [54]

The BRIDE *appears. Her orange blossom has gone, and
she is wearing a black shawl.*

NEIGHBOUR   *angrily, to her*   Why in God's name have
you come here?

BRIDE   Where else could I go?

MOTHER   *to the* NEIGHBOUR   Who is it?

NEIGHBOUR   Don't you know who it is?

MOTHER   That's why I ask. Because if I did know I'd
sink my teeth into her throat. Snake!   *She rushes at
the* BRIDE, *but stops short. To the* NEIGHBOUR.   Look
at her. There she is crying, and I just stand here
without tearing her eyes out. I don't understand.
Do you think I just didn't love him enough?   *To
the* BRIDE.   Where's your precious honour now?
Where is it?   *She strikes the* BRIDE, *who falls to the
ground.* [55]

NEIGHBOUR   For God's sake!   *She tries to separate them.*

BRIDE   *to the* NEIGHBOUR   Leave her; I came here for her
to kill me, so that they can take me with them.   *To
the* MOTHER.   But not with your bare hands; with
shears, with a sickle, with anything that can shred
my bones. Leave her be! I want her to know that I'm
clean, that she can kill me and bury me, but that no

man has ever seen himself in the whiteness of my breasts.

MOTHER   What do I care about that?

BRIDE   Because I went with him . . . I went with him. *Full of anguish.*   And you would have gone too. I was a woman burning, covered in sores inside and out, and your son was a trickle of water which would give me children, land, health, but he was a dark river, full of branches, filling me with the murmur of its reeds, singing to me through clenched teeth. And I ran with your son, with your little boy of cold water, and the other one followed me with flocks of birds, so that I couldn't even walk, and my flesh filled with frost, the wounded flesh of a woman already withering, of a young girl burning. Listen to me well, I didn't want to, I didn't want to, do you hear? . . I didn't want to. Your son was all I ever wished for, and I didn't betray him, but the other one sucked me in with the force of the sea, and nothing could ever have stopped me from going . . . not ever, not even if I'd been old and all your son's children were holding me by the hair.

Another NEIGHBOUR *enters.*

MOTHER   So it's not her fault . . . and not mine either! *Sarcastic.*   Whose fault is it then? What sort of whore leaves her wedding to jump into the corner of a bed warmed by another woman?

BRIDE   No, no . . . Take your revenge. Look how soft my throat is; you could cut it as easily as a dahlia in your garden. But that's not true. I'm as clean and as pure as a new-born baby. And with the strength to prove it. Light a fire, and we'll put our hands into the flame; you for your son, me for my body. You'll be the first to take them out.

Another NEIGHBOUR *enters.*

MOTHER   What does your body matter to me? What
    does whether you live or die matter to me? What
    does anything matter? Nothing matters but the
    wheat my sons lie under and the rain that washes
    their faces, and God himself who has laid them to
    rest.

Another NEIGHBOUR *enters.*

BRIDE   Let me cry with you.

MOTHER   Cry if you want. But do it at the door.

GIRL 3 *comes in. The* BRIDE *stands in the doorway. The*
    MOTHER *is in the centre of the stage.*

WIFE   *entering towards the left*
    He was the finest of horsemen
    and now just melting snow.
    He rode through fairs and mountains
    and women's arms.
    And now just moss and night
    caress his face.

MOTHER
    Sunflower of Mother Sun,
    mirror of earth.
    Let them put a cross
    of bitter oleander on your breast,
    a sheet of shining silk
    to cover you,
    let the water weep
    between your still hands.

WIFE
    And now four boys come
    with their shoulders heavy.

BRIDE
    Four young boys
    carry death through the air.

MOTHER
 Neighbours.

GIRL 3   *in the doorway*
 They're bringing them now.

MOTHER
 When makes no difference.
 The cross. The cross.

WOMEN
 Sweet nails,
 sweet cross.
 Sweet name
 of Jesus.[56]

BRIDE
 May the cross shelter the living and the dead.

MOTHER
 Neighbours, it was with a knife,
 just a little knife,
 that on the appointed day between two and three,
 two men in love killed each other.
 With a knife,
 just a little knife,
 that fits snug in the hand
 and slices so quickly
 through the startled flesh
 to stop at the point
 where the dark root of the scream
 lies trembling enmeshed.

BRIDE
 And this is a knife,
 just a little knife,
 that fits snug in the hand,
 a fish without scales,
 a fish without river,
 so that on the appointed day between two and three,
 two men lie stiff,
 with their lips turning yellow.

MOTHER

       It fits so snug in the hand,
       but slices so quick
       through the startled flesh
       and there it stops, at the point
       where, trembling enmeshed,
       lies the dark root of the scream.

       The NEIGHBOURS *weep, kneeling on the floor.*

       Curtain.

Notes

1   The original Spanish here refers to 'drag-hoes and winnowing-forks'. The change to 'the sickle and the scythe', however, is not as arbitrary as it may seem. On one hand, whilst admittedly losing the specifically rustic connotations of these instruments, it also avoids their clumsy sounds and, indeed, their perhaps faintly comic overtones. Lorca frequently chooses certain objects out of a multiplicity of possibilities, all of which would suit his meaning, primarily to satisfy the demands of musicality and rhythm. The translator must do the same. What is really important here is the way in which the knife has suddenly been transformed from a simple domestic utensil into a source of threat to human life which is present in every sphere of activity (hence the subsequent reference to the accident which has befallen Rafael). In terms of a grammar of images, the use of the 'sickle and the scythe' is wholly faithful to both the rhythmic force and the intention of the original.

2   *Blood Wedding* is structured on a whole series of dualist images which speak of apparently positive values (the bull here being equated to strength) whilst simultaneously foreshadowing destruction (in Spain the fighting-bull is bred solely to die).

3   The original Spanish – 'vieja, revieja, requetevieja' – is a fine example of the delight that Lorca takes in playful, highly rhythmical language. In this case, it is impossible to reproduce anything much beyond the sense that the Mother is letting herself become old before her time.

4   A common device in Lorca's theatre is the creation of phrases which have a proverbial ring (thereby intensifying the sense of a community voice), but which are in fact original. The original Spanish – 'Men, men; wheat, wheat' – echoes the proverb 'bread, bread; wine, wine', meaning 'to call a spade a spade' and stresses the natural and inviolable order of things. The fact that it depends on the linguistic frame of reference of its audience for its success means that a literal English translation is impossible.

5   The original – 'When do you want me to ask for her?' – is a reference to the contractual arrangements which placed social formalities over individual rights.

6   The very typical exclamation 'Ay!' (pronounced 'I') is commonly used in Spanish to express every emotion from surprise to sudden pain. It is frequently used by performers of deep song and flamenco.

7   At the heart of the Mother's fear is what is known in Spanish as the 'el que dirán', meaning basically 'what folk will say'. In a society in which, historically, the slightest slur on character could lead to an unpleasant confrontation with the Inquisition, an unblemished reputation was essential to be able to maintain one's position within the status quo. This is an early echo of the obsession with reputation which drives Bernarda Alba.

8   The Spanish has 'Your son is worth a lot'. This is a reference to his social position and reputation, and with it the Neighbour is justifying the strength of the Mother's concern.

9   The original has 'Leonardo of the Felix family', thereby creating the sense of a whole clan which is feuding with the family of the Mother. It is also worth noting that Leonardo is the only principal character of the play to be given a name, the others being cast only in terms of function rather than individuality. Leonardo suggests 'burning lion', a clear reference to his passionate nature, while Felix provides both a generic surname, in that it refers to 'cats', and also echoes the Spanish 'feliz', meaning 'happy'. Lorca is clearly implying that Leonardo belongs to a different 'breed' of person.

10   The central imagery of the entire play is condensed into this song. In this case, the dualist opposition of blood/water (passion/marriage; death/life) is being set out. The horse rejects water because of what we might call in English 'the call of the blood'.

11   'Snow' (and its associated meanings) is introduced here as one of the central emblems of the play. In emblematic terms, it can be understood in this way: to avoid burning with passion, Leonardo has tried to freeze out his feelings. Thus, in the wedding songs, the reference to the Bride's 'blouse of shining snow' is another dualist image – the whiteness of purity, the freezing reality of self–repression. It is also a foreshadowing of the coldness of death and is used explicitly in that sense in the final act of the play.

12   This idea of the horse running 'to his young mare's side' is a clear echo of Leonardo's constant journeys on horseback to the Bride's house. He is seen at the end of Act 1 and makes

specific reference to these journeys in the forest scene, so that the horse becomes wholly identified with the animal part of Leonardo's nature that brings him to rebel against convention.

13   The identification of Leonardo with the horse is established from his first appearance. In this case, the mention of 'sharp stones' echoes the 'wounded hooves' of the lullaby horse.

14   This is an emblematic way of telling the audience that Leonardo is 'a man on fire'. It is this type of concerted structure of emblems and references which gives *Blood Wedding* its tight dramatic and linguistic cohesion. The fact that he is drinking lemon is, therefore, an image of the bitterness of his life. The parallel is firmly established when the Bride refers to the bitterness of her impending wedding at the start of Act 2.

15   There have been attempts to situate Lorca's plays outside Spain, most commonly in Celtic communities – the most successful example of this being Frank McGuinness's lyrical translation of *Yerma* into Northern Irish speech. However, it is equally valid to insist upon the very Spanish roots of this universal tragedy without necessarily turning the piece into an exercise in stage–Spanishness.

16   The original reads 'Two fine fortunes are joining together'. This introduces the suggestion that materialistic considerations underlie society's celebration of this marriage. The important sense that it is money that is 'joining' in marriage rather than people is conveyed by the translation's use of the common phrase that 'money breeds money'. The goal and fruit of such unions in this society are not life-orientated, but are rather geared towards profit and material advancement.

17   The Mother-in-Law literally echoes Leonardo's words in the original, simply ordering her daughter to 'shut up!'. In the context, this jars in English. However, the translation attempts to convey the same basic sense of injustice in that the Mother-in-Law calls for her daughter not to question either Leonardo's authority or his motives.

18   The Bride is described as living in a 'cave'. This has deliberate overtones of the gypsy families who live in caves on the Sacromonte in Granada, and as such carries suggestions of both personal pride (the Bride and her Mother) and comparative poverty (hence, the Father's veiled insistence that he cannot give a dowry). The divisive influence of money on

human relationships is attacked by Lorca in other works, notably *The House of Bernarda Alba*. In the case of *Blood Wedding* it is the prime mover of the tragedy in that it was economic considerations which originally came between Leonardo and the Bride.

19   The mention of the Jupiter plant (which, strictly speaking, is probably the orpine or house-leek in English) is an emblematic reference to the transient glory of life. Significantly, it is the only flower the Mother mentions and, equally significantly, it is the one which dries up and dies (in the way that both Leonardo and the Bride are metaphorically 'burnt'). The plant also provides a very appropriate image of the sudden flaring into life of the passion of Leonardo and the Bride because it grows through stone walls (see note 22).

20   In the original the Bride is described as rising to prepare the traditional Andalusian breakfast, served to men about to go to the fields, of bread crumbs, usually left to soak overnight, fried in olive oil and garlic. The closest cultural equivalent in English is probably baking bread.

21   Instead of 'full of hopes', the original Spanish has 'macho'. When the Mother uses this word she is suggesting that, as a young male endowed with all the aura of fertility that we have already seen her associate with the 'macho', her dead son had a glowing future before him. However, for a contemporary English-speaking audience, any reference to 'macho' or 'manliness' would spark a different set of resonances.

22   The basic idea that men work the fields while women stay indoors permits Lorca to use the idea of the wall as an emblem of a society which, literally, hides its women away and, metaphorically, locks away its true feelings.

23   The mention of a 'stray runner from the herd' not only serves to heighten the identification of Leonardo with the horse, but is also a clear indication that his passion has brought him to the point of breaking free from community restraint. In this sense, it echoes Martirio's description of the rebellious Adela in *The House of Bernarda Alba* as 'a young mule still to be broken in'.

24   Lorca frequently uses the notion of predestination in his plays to convey his brooding sense of final pessimism. Quite clearly, this sense of fatalism weighs heavily upon the whole structure of *Blood Wedding*. Indeed, it is against this impending sense of destruction that Lorca focuses the life-force incarnate

in the runaway lovers (creating the same tension that he saw in the world around him and in life itself). Rather than taking this feeling of being predestined to failure as forming part of a coherent system of belief, however, it would be more accurate to view it as a poeticisation of Lorca's lingering sense that the odds are firmly stacked against human happiness.

25   The bird is considered an archetypal symbol of female sexuality, and Lorca uses it in this way throughout his work. In this case, and in the re-appearance of the nightingale in Girl 3's speech towards the end of the final scene, the bird is a symbol of life at its most lyrical.

26   In the original Leonardo says simply 'The bride! She must be happy!'. The English translation tries to capture the same sense of cliché behind which Leonardo conceals his mounting frustration.

27   The whole of the wedding scene is structured around the voice of the community urging the hesitant Bride towards full acceptance of the social contract of marriage. Coming as it does in the middle of this particularly tense confrontation, it serves as a primary coercive element.

28   Leonardo describes himself literally as a 'man of blood'.

29   The original Spanish reads here 'When things reach their centres, nobody can pluck them out'. The image of the 'water rising in an unstoppable well' is an attempt to re-create the sense of folk wisdom of the original, and is 'borrowed' from an early Pablo Neruda poem.

30   The Spanish refers specifically to a 'bottle of anisette' and 'a quilt of roses'. Clearly, the idea of a 'bed of roses' would be misleading in English and the leap from 'anisette' to 'sweet wine' is hardly an audacious one.

31   In this repetition of the words sung by the incoming guests, the Bride is echoing one of the central notions of Spanish Golden Age theatre, namely, the need to arouse oneself from the treacherous dream of the senses.

32   As with the lullaby sung by the Wife and the Mother-in-Law, the wedding songs contain double-edged images which speak, in this case, of marital and natural plenitude at the same time as they contribute to a growing sense of fatalism. The image of the wheel here suggests both the fulfilment and the passing of life.

33   The maid here is staging her own version of the marriage ritual, and it is noticeable how easily religious imagery

(especially the reference to the Bridegroom as the 'dove with a burning heart of fire') merges with a more sensual tone, culminating in the traditional celebration of the blood which betokens the loss of female virginity. The final exhortation to the Bride to 'make the water glow' immediately brings back into play the opposition of water/blood.

34   Instead of 'crystal cup', the Spanish has 'monstrance'. Once again, this implies just how thin the veneer of religiosity is in this society.

35   During the whole of the wedding scene, Leonardo becomes a brooding presence, constantly coming and going. His evident frustration and the Bride's growing nervousness are highlighted against the wedding which, by this time, has become virtually a character in its own right.

36   The Spanish says literally 'Dances from beyond the shore of the sea', implying that those dancing have a more liberated view of life. The translation given here has an echo of Yeats's 'The Fiddler of Dooney'.

37   Both the Maid's previous speech and the Bridegroom's reply have been invested with a touch of the theatrical innuendo that one normally finds at weddings. It is perfectly valid in the case of the Maid's playful allusion to the forthcoming wedding night. In the case of the Bridegroom, the change from 'the bride' to 'my wife' is an attempt to get round the difficult problem posed throughout the play by the use of the word 'novia', which can mean anything from a serious girlfriend through fiancée to bride.

38   The fact that it is the wedding pins which bring matters to a head for the Bride echoes Leonardo's subsequent declaration in the woods that 'the silver pins of your wedding turned my blood black'. The pins are also clearly reminiscent of the knife and so become part of the build-up of the sense of inevitable violence and death.

39   The Mother says literally, 'It's the preparation of the earth and the plantation of new trees'. The translation seeks to capture the rhythm of the original by substituting the rather clumsy nouns with present participles. The central idea behind the Mother's words is that marriage is an integral part of the natural world, ensuring growth across the generations. If we make the equation of Mother = Earth then, clearly, a very passive role is being assigned to the woman.

40   This speech is important not only because it gives an

insight into the Mother's influence over the Bridegroom, but also because it suggests that the whole feeling of fatalism which presides over the characters springs largely from the way in which one generation inherits from the previous one those same strict codes of behaviour and authoritarian attitudes which, later on, will not hesitate to condemn Leonardo and the Bride.

41   The original Spanish describes the lovers as fleeing 'hugging each other, like an exhalation'. The translation of 'riding like the wind' conveys some sense of the surging relief of freedom.

42   The Woodcutters have an essentially choral function here, symbolising above all the conflict of the forces of life and death which the flight of Leonardo and the Bride has unleashed.

43   These words are an echo of the Father's earlier declaration to the Mother that 'What's mine is hers and what's yours is his'. In this case the sense is of a union of love rather than of a contractual arrangement.

44   Like the knife at the start of the play, the Moon is introduced in an apparently casual manner.

45   The moon's association with death is a constant in the work of Lorca. In this case, the Moon's lust for blood and appetite for death make of it the incarnation of the darkest elements in human life. It also presides, like an evil eye, over the ritualistic slaying of the lover and jilted bridegroom. It is appropriate that the Moon should be played by a 'young Woodcutter with a white face', partly because this adds to the Moon's sexual ambivalence (the moon is traditionally seen as feminine), partly because it reinforces the idea that the Moon is a poetic embodiment of the dominant force of violence (which the knife symbolises and of which the Woodcutters are painfully aware) which has been pulsing throughout the play.

46   The translation adds the comparison 'like fish' to reinforce the apparent autonomy of the knives. The likening of 'knife' to 'fish' occurs in the Bride's final speech, and also in several of Lorca's poems.

47   It is important to note that, at this stage anyway, Leonardo and the Bride still haven't entirely deadened the community voice of violent disapproval implanted inside them by the whole process of socialisation. This explains the images of mutilation and confusion in the speeches of both characters, as well as accounting for the abrupt changes in the

Bride's attitudes towards Leonardo. Significantly, the Bride refers here to the 'metal chain' she feels Leonardo has placed around her neck (later on, when speaking to the Mother, she will once again speak of her helplessness in resisting the pull of Leonardo). This is her version of Leonardo's 'It's not me who's to blame, it's the earth itself'. Both characters' confession of impotence in the face of the tidal pull of passion is, generally speaking, the last vestige of an inculcated conscience and, specifically, their attempt at finding some sort of answer to Leonardo's conviction, stated just before the wedding, that 'there's always blame'.

48   Leonardo's fear that dawn is about to break represents the final victory of the Moon, which has already defined itself in terms of three images of falseness, the final one being 'false dawn on the leaves'.

49   This is a reference to the traditional public airing of the bride's sheets after the wedding night.

50   The colours blue and red here are clear references to the normal manner of representing veins and arteries. Moreover, the wool itself stands for the course of human life, always finite, always liable to be cut. The dramatic leap from violent death to the children's game with which the final scene opens is certainly a considerable one, but it serves to reinforce the sense of the omnipresence of death.

51   Characteristically, at the end of the play Lorca directs the full force of his compassion at the women who are left to pick up whatever pieces they can. In this case, the Wife must lock herself away, as if in perpetual mourning or lost in undying shame, for the rest of her days. In point of fact, this was more or less the fate of the real bride after the events in Níjar which inspired the play.

52   The fateful inevitability of the events, expressed by the Beggarwoman's 'The way it had to be' ('It was the most fitting thing', in the original), is yet another forceful expression of Lorca's combined sense of pessimism and outrage.

53   This is an explicit echo of the *duende* which flows from the 'soles of the feet' and another emblematic reminder that the source of our emotions, for better and for worse, resides more in our animal nature rather than our civilised persona.

54   This particularly powerful speech reveals how deeply ingrained the whole question of social appearances is in the Mother. The final image echoes the language of the beggar

who hasn't a single crust of bread to raise to his or her mouth. In a society obsessed with façade, at least in the way that Lorca saw it, poverty of any type is socially unacceptable.

55   The actual Spanish of the Mother's final reference to honour here is ambiguous because she is talking about her son and referring to the Bride in the third person. The fact that the Neighbour is acting as a sort of intermediary between Mother and Bride, and that immediately after finishing this speech the Mother physically attacks the Bride, suggests that the words are directed at her. In this sense, the Mother once again becomes the voice of tradition, taunting the young woman in front of her with her loss of reputation. This is certainly the way in which the Bride understands it, as her reply makes clear. Her justification of her action to the Mother, one of the most powerful pieces of writing in the whole of Lorca's theatre, returns to the earlier notion of the individual's helplessness in resisting the force of passion. But the striking question, of course, is why, under these circumstances, she should be concerned at all with trying to rescue her reputation. It is the final illustration of just how deeply ingrained the voice of society is within us all.

56   It is significant that the play does not end on an image of religious consolation (indeed, the fact that the women's prayer contains a specific reference to nails, part of the structure of images associated with the knife, means that it is also pervaded by a sense of inevitably violent death). This moment of apparent religious serenity is presented almost as a mechanical bowing of the head in the direction of what is socially acceptable rather than metaphysically possible. The final words of the women quickly bring the spectator back to the contemplation of the knife and the timeless scream of human horror in the face of the transience of life and love.

Brief Chronology of Lorca's Life

1898 In the same year as Spain lost Cuba, the last vestige of its once immense American empire, Federico García Lorca was born in Fuentevaqueros, in the province of Granada, son of Federico García Rodríquez and Vicenta Lorca Romero.

1908 He begins to study piano. Music was to remain one of the abiding passions of his life, and for many years he thought seriously of becoming a professional musician.

1914 Goes to the University of Granada to study Law, where he was described as 'not a particularly brilliant' student.

1917 Strikes up friendships with two older men which are to have important repercussions for his subsequent career. The composer Manuel de Falla stimulates his interest in the musical roots of Andalusia, and the socialist Professor of Law, Fernando de los Ríos is responsible for encouraging him to develop his literary talents.

1918 Publishes his first book *Impressions and Landscapes* (prose). He begins to write his first published poems. [As Lorca often took years to work through a subject, and was notoriously loath to commit his poems and plays to the printed page, this chronology gives, where appropriate, only the date of publication or first performance of specific works.]

1919 Following the advice of Fernando de los Ríos, Lorca goes to live in the Residencia de Estudiantes, in Madrid, where he subsequently meets Luis Buñuel, Salvador Dalí, and many of the brilliant poets with whom he will come to form the so-called Generation of '27.

1920 Unsuccessful production of *The Butterfly's Evil Spell*.

1921 Publication of *Book of Poems*.

1922 Organises a festival of deep song, jointly with Falla, in the Alhambra, Granada.

1923–27 Period of intense activity, in which Lorca writes both plays and poetry. During this time he also cements his friendship with Dalí.

1927 Publication of the book of poetry *Songs*. His play *Mariana Pineda*, with set design by Salvador Dalí, receives its first performance in Barcelona. Lorca has his first exhibition of drawings, also in Barcelona.

1928 Publication of *Gypsy Ballads*, to enormous public and critical acclaim. Dalí, however, criticises the work. This initiates a period of personal depression in Lorca, as well as heralding the beginning of the disintegration of the relationship between Lorca, Dalí and Buñuel.

1929 His one-act play *The Love of don Perlimplin for Belisa in the Garden* is halted in rehearsals by the censor of the Primo de Rivera dictatorship. Lorca sets sail to New York.

1930 Returns to Spain via Cuba. First performance of *The Shoemaker's Wonderful Wife*.

1931 Finishes writing *The Public*, which he reads to shocked friends. Considered Lorca's most intimate play, it did not receive its first professional performance until 1986. In the same year he finally publishes *Poem of Deep Song*, written ten years earlier. Fernando de los Ríos, now Minister of Education, approves Lorca's idea for the creation of a travelling theatre company. La Barraca is born and Lorca dedicates himself wholeheartedly to its work. That summer, however, in a two-week burst of almost frenzied creativity, Lorca writes *Blood Wedding*.

1933 First performance of *Blood Wedding* to great acclaim. Spends the last few months of the year in Argentina (where *Blood Wedding* is also performed, once again with marked success) and establishes a firm friendship with the Chilean poet, Pablo Neruda.

1934 His close friend, Ignacio Sánchez Mejías, is gored in the bull ring and subsequently dies. Lorca is moved to write the masterly 'Lament for Ignacio Sánchez Mejías', one of the finest poems in the Spanish language. At the same time, as political tension intensifies in the country, especially with General Franco's brutal repression of the Asturian miners' strike, Lorca becomes more and more politically active. The enormously successful première of *Yerma*, in December of that year, is interrupted by right-wing elements.

1935   Writes the play *Doña Rosita, the Spinster* and begins work on *Sonnets of Dark Love*, neither of which was to be published in his lifetime.

1936   Lorca's last year of life begins with the publication of *Blood Wedding* and the book of poems *First Songs*, written nearly fourteen years earlier. As Spanish society becomes increasingly polarised, Lorca firmly nails his political colours to the mast, and participates in several anti-fascist rallies. He finishes *The House of Bernarda Alba* not long before setting off for Granada to celebrate his saint's day with his family on 18 July. Just as he is leaving Madrid he entrusts several important manuscripts to friends, including *Poet in New York* and the surrealistic play *Just as Soon as Five Years Pass*. Lorca is arrested on 16 August by Ramón Ruiz Alonso and, despite interventions by Manuel de Falla and the poet Luis Rosales, is executed just outside the village of Viznar on 19 August, on the direct orders of General Queipo de Llano, Military Governor of Seville. His body was thrown into an unmarked grave.